GENERA

BUSES
OF THE TWENTIES

An introduction to
the K, S, NS, LS classes

GEORGE ROBBINS

IMAGES PUBLISHING
(MALVERN) LTD

First published in Great Britain 1996 by
IMAGES PUBLISHING (MALVERN) LTD.

in conjunction with
JOHN A. S. HAMBLEY
7 Linden Road,
Dunstable
Beds. LU5 4NZ

British Library Cataloguing in Publication Data

A catalogue record for this book is available
from the British Library

ISBN 1 897817 73 8

Designed and Produced by Images Publishing (Malvern) Ltd.
The Wells House, Holywell Road, Malvern Wells, Worcestershire.

Printed and Bound in Great Britain by Bookcraft, Bath, Avon.

CONTENTS

ACKNOWLEDGEMENTS

I have had an enormous amount of encouragement and support whilst writing this book so it is hard to know where the thanks should begin.

However, I would like to single out for a special thank you, Norman Anscomb, who first put forward the idea for the book and who has vigorously pushed the project through to its conclusion.

A further thank you is also extended to Brian Bunker, John Cummings, Andrew Gilks, Reg Westgate and the London Historical Research Group of the Omnibus Society to which reference has been made for checking certain details.

The front and back cover illustrations were provided by Ian MacDonald to which a special thankyou is extended.

Photographs used are from many sources, acknowledged where known, though a considerable number are from unknown employees of the General.

K672 transferred to the Cambrian fleet on 21 December 1926 is seen here working on route 185B a weekday service between Liverpool Street Station and Shepherds Bush (Askew Crescent). It has been taken over by demonstrators supporting the miners.

THE STORY OF THE
AEC K TYPE BUS

By January 1919 after four years of war the motor bus fleet of the London General Omnibus Company was greatly depleted and only one thousand nine hundred and seventy five B type buses remained in service – although some seven hundred buses had been added to the fleet during 1919 including two hundred and fifty new B type and a number of the older ones relicensed the time had come for an improvement in the style of London buses. This was the K type which was an important "landmark" in the story of the motor bus. It was the first bus to break away from the long accepted layout of a bus, viz – engine, drivers cab and body. It marked the end of the horse-bus influence on motor bus design which had seldom permitted the carrying of more than thirty four passengers, sixteen inside and eighteen outside.

The K type changed all this by placing the driver beside the engine and a somewhat wider straight sided body enabled the seating capacity to be increased to 46 passengers, being 22 inside and 24 outside. The new style of body also made it possible for transverse seats to be provided on the lower deck a practice which hitherto had only been fitted to a few experimental buses and some single deckers. This forward-control type of bus became the standard for A.E.C. passenger vehicles and subsequently for the majority of buses built since that time.

Although the K type bus was not seen much outside the London area, the heavier S and PS types which soon followed were to be seen throughout the country. This revolutionary type of chassis had been designed in 1911 by the LGOC but development and production had been held up by the 1914/18 war and it was not till August 1919 that K1 was finally completed, and ready for road tests, as the following extracts from a report in Modern Transport of 16th August 1919 shows:-

"A NEW TYPE OF OMNIBUS FOR LONDON"

We are now enabled to supplement the particulars given in an earlier issue relative to the new type of omnibus of the LGOC by some further information of the vehicle as submitted for road tests on August 11. The vehicle, built by the Associated Equipment Company Ltd., has a length overall of 22ft. 9ins. width of 7ft. 1½ins. height 12ft. 6ins. height inside of 6ft. length of platform 4ft. wheel base 14ft. 2¼ins. The passenger carrying capacity is 22 inside and 24 outside, compared with 16 inside and 18 outside on the existing type of L.G.O.C. bus. The additional body space has been secured by extending the front end to the position occupied by the dashboard in the older type and by bringing the sides down straight to the floor instead of curving them inwards as previously. An innovation of the electric lighting equipment is that the lamp boxes are let into the forward and rear canopies for the driver and conductor and they are so arranged as to shine in a downward direction and upwards to the destination board. Increased accommodation for passengers is gained through saving the space that the driver at present occupies between the bonnet and the body of the vehicle. The bonnet is built up to the front of the omnibus itself, and the driver sits on the right-hand side in a recess cut in the bonnet and protected by a shield. He sits higher up, and as the exhaust gases escape on the left-hand side, he is much cooler than on the older type. The steering is also much easier.

K221 was one of the buses fitted with a new curved or turn under style body in 1925. It is seen here working from Chelverton Road, Putney (AF) garage (during its stay there from 9 September to 16 November 1925) on route 37A Peckham to Isleworth.

The omnibuses are well sprung and comfortably upholstered inside, and the running is very smooth. Except for two short seats by the door which face each other, the inside seats face forwards. Instead of straps there are four brass rods from floor to ceiling to enable passengers to get in and out easily. It is not expected that standing inside will be allowed, as this was only a war-time concession by the police. The top is built so as to come slightly over the driver.

One of the chief changes is the increased width of the platform and the stairs. There is no danger of a jerk of the omnibus throwing one over the stair rail into the road, for the new stairs are more like those of the tramway cars. The platform is wide enough, as in the trams for two streams of people to get in or out of it, although the actual increase in width is only 14 in. There is an electric bell; and the slightest touch on the cord or on the bell-push upstairs is sufficient to ring it – a great improvement especially for outside travellers. The speed of the omnibus is 12 miles an hour. When production is in full swing the vehicles will probably be turned out at the rate of fifty a week.

The test to which the omnibus was put by the police was carried out on the main Portsmouth Road. The omnibus has to ascend a one in 25 gradient on second speed at not less than 12 or more than 16 miles an hour, and the steeper gradients at four miles an hour. The brake test requires that the bus can be pulled up in double its own length when going at fair speed.

The AEC specification quoted it as a 30 h.p. chassis fitted with a four cylinder engine, 100 mm bore x 140 mm stroke. It had multiplate clutch and chain gearbox. Rear axle ratio 8¼ to 1. The weight was 4tons 4cwt. Although the type was given AEC classification 301 and later developments as 302 to 305 the chassis were numbered on from K 1 which was 20001. The first two or possibly three K type chassis were built in 1919 and K1 entered service in London in August 1919 on route 11 Shepherds Bush and Liverpool Street, K2 followed in September and this was sent to Seven Kings garage for route 25 Victoria and Seven Kings. Both may have operated on other routes as a photograph shows K2 on the 32, Turnham Green and Wimbledon Common. K3 was used as an instructional chassis and was not fitted with a bus body until 1928 when it was put to use as a survey vehicle and given registration number UC 2221.

K2 was sent to Seven Kings (AP) garage in September 1919 for service on route 25. Note the narrow driver's shields on K1 and K2. K2 was withdrawn in October 1920 and sold to A.E.C.

It was some eight months before any more K type buses came into service and then they appeared in a steady flow from May 1920 until May 1921. A total of one thousand and forty K type chassis were produced during this period and the trade press made special mention of the production of the 1000th K type bus. These K type buses were allocated to many of the main central London routes thus releasing the older B type buses for new routes in and around London.

This main delivery of K type chassis were in three batches, K4 – 503, K504-1003 and K1004-1043. The first two hundred bodies were built by the LGOC at their North Road body works. Many more were built by other body builders, 300 by Short Bros 285 by Brush and 100 by Strachan. The remainder by the LGOC at North Road or Seagrave Road. All bodies were to the same standard design.

K391 of Leyton (T) garage on route 38 stands alongside an S type probably from Palmers Green (AD) garage on route 29, at Victoria Station.

Note in this interior lower deck view of K413 the fleet number painted on the staircase, and the Leyland LB visible on the left hand side. This K was one of those drafted to the Cambrian fleet at Hanwell (HW) garage in April 1927. It returned to the LGOC fleet in April 1928 and had only one further operational move to Dalston (D) garage in March 1930. It was delicensed into Muswell Hill (MH) garage at the end of November 1930 and sold to Cohen in February 1931. (London Transport U6262)

K1 and K2 were given registration numbers LU 8231 and 8232 and the others followed with registration numbers between LU 8233 and 8600, XC 8001 and 8500, XC 9701 and 9800 and XF 8001-84. A small number of other members of the class received registration identifications outside these ranges

They appeared and were registered in a most erratic order and many early numbers which would have been expected in May 1920 did not appear until a year later. These late comers included K11, 26, 34, 200, 308, 344 and 346. Another late one was K139 which for a time had carried a lorry body. Possibly the same may have applied to K181 which was not fitted with a bus body and registered until late in 1923 when it was registered as XP 4181.

During July 1921 a further nineteen K type buses were built and entered service, these being K1044 to 1062 and that was the highest number for some time as I well remember noting in those years. By this time K type buses had been allocated to the following garages , B (Battersea), D (Dalston), G (Forest Gate), H (Hackney), J (Holloway), N (Norwood), P (Old Kent Road), Q (Camberwell), R (Hammersmith), X (Middle Row), AC (Willesden), AD (Palmers Green), AE (Hendon), AL (Merton), AM (Plumstead), AP (Seven Kings), AR (Tottenham) and CF (Chalk Farm). Seven Kings with nearly 100 vehicles was all K type as was Hackney with 60 buses, but the others had B type buses as well and many garages had no K type buses at this time. I am not certain of the order of allocation except that the last four garages to receive the new buses in 1921 were Willesden, Battersea, Hackney and Camberwell. I remember the last named having these new buses as they used to work on route 78 and I noted K1009 to 1042 operating from Q garage at that time. The other routes which had K type buses in those days were 2, 3, 6, 7, 10, 11, 13, 15, 19, 21, 25, 29, 32, 35, 42, 53, 77, 77A, 88 and 107. Most of these routes are familiar today and are easily recognised except maybe the 32, which was then Turnham Green and Wimbledon Common, 42, Finsbury Park and Camberwell Green and 107, Clapham Common and Dorking. There were frequent changes in the allocation of the K type buses at that time as the larger 54 seat S type bus had been introduced in December 1920 and came into full production during 1921/2. The S type replaced the Ks on many of the important cross London routes and the displaced K type then went to other garages and routes to replace the B type. Further new S type and then the more advanced NS type arrived in 1923 and so the K type moved from route to route and garage to garage making it impossible to recount the changes. Suffice it to say that K type buses must have worked on practically all double deck routes in London and have been operated from all garages at some time during those years.

LU 8375 K 260 was loaned to East Surrey between June 1923 and October 1929. It carries both the K number of its owner and the East Surrey fleet number 86. The route S2B operated from Sidcup to Farnborough from August 1921 until it was renumbered 411 in December 1924. In lack of a garage, the vehicles were originally operated from the Railway Hotel in Sevenoaks. (Snook)

The majority of the K type chassis built passed to the LGOC and only about thirty went elsewhere. Six were sold in 1920 to Torquay Tramways who operated them in that seaside town as feeders to the trams and they passed later to Devon General. Another twelve were purchased by the East Surrey Traction Company and were painted in their then blue livery. They were in two batches, first six in 1920 having London XB registrations and the others new early in 1921 and registered in Surrey as PB 9558-63.

In August 1920 K232 was returned to AEC who sold it to Robinsons of Scarborough and it was relicenced as NO 2114. This no doubt led Robinson to purchase further K type as in January 1922 they had AJ 7584 and AJ 7587. This was followed by XB 9084, a single deck which had been a demonstrator. The AEC had fitted a K type with a single deck body and right hand drive for exhibition at a Roads Congress at The Hague, Holland in September 1920. Two chassis, numbers 20588 and 20589 were fitted with double deck bodies 5339 and 5346 and sold to AEC on the 31st December 1920 as no doubt they had a purchaser in mind. Nothing much is known of another five chassis retained by AEC except that one had registration number LF 9243 and another a little later as XH 3021. Another fifteen K type entered service in May 1924 numbered K1063-1077. They had been built up at Chiswick Works and were identical to the earlier buses. These 15 buses were all allocated to Cricklewood garage when new, working mainly on route 16 between Cricklewood "The Crown" and Victoria.

Until 1923 all these K type buses were operated by the LGOC on their own routes and under the fleet name of "General". In June 1923 thirty K type buses were transferred to East Surrey to work on some routes in Kent and Surrey which this Company operated on behalf of General. They were painted red and had "East Surrey" on the sides and were in addition to the twelve K type owned by East Surrey which were then re-painted red.

During the same year some K type buses were transferred to two other General subsidiaries. One was the Tramways (MET) Omnibus Company Ltd. and some one hundred and thirty K type buses were transferred from General to replace B type vehicles. This company used the fleet name "Metropolitan" and they worked on certain specified routes such as 28, 30, 37, 48 (Golders Green – Blackheath) 74 etc. These routes were operated from various General garages. Nine other K type buses were transferred to the South Metropolitan Electric Tramways who ran under the name of "Southern". These were later absorbed into the Metropolitan fleet which eventually had a total of one hundred and sixty two K type buses.

A new development occurred in 1925 when the single deck version of the K type bus appeared. Up to that time General single deck routes were worked by B or S type single deckers. It also introduced the first pneumatic tyred bus to London. Twenty four new K type chassis were built and were numbered K1078-1101. They had new 24 seat single deck bodies to a rather attractive design. The first six appeared in August 1925 and were put on a new route 162, between Slough and Leatherhead, a route which later developed into country area route 462. They were operated from a new small garage at Slough, code (SL). Three of these buses when new, were allocated to another of the LGOC's associated companies, the National Omnibus and Transport Co who operated routes in the North of London. These three buses were K1096-98 and they had Hertfordshire registration numbers RO 2072-2070.

K196 is shown working from South Harrow (SH) garage opened on 15 April 1925 and closed on 9 April 1930 when Harrow Weald (HD) garage opened. Note the driver is wearing his white summer coat and both he and the conductor have white tops to their caps, worn by all bus crews in the summer months.

K808 and NS1316 stand outside Streatham (AK) garage awaiting crews before they take up service on route 49A which ran beyond Crystal Palace to Lewisham from 21 January 1920 to 30 November 1924. As NS1316 was delivered new to Streatham in May 1924, the picture was probably taken during the summer of 1924.
(E G Masterman)

Early in 1926 another twenty five of these single deck buses were ordered together with the same number of chassis from AEC these being K1102-1126. But these chassis and the bodies ordered for them never met, as the bodies were ready some eight or nine months before the chassis. So these new single deck bodies were mounted on older K type chassis from which the double deck bodies had been removed. They ranged over the whole series from K45 to K1053.

Between June 1926 and April 1927 another seventy nine of these single deck bodies were built but no new chassis were ordered for them and they were all mounted on a similar number of older K type chassis again displacing double deck bodies. The single deck K type were of varying seating capacities and not all had pneumatics. There were thirty three with 24 seat bodies and pneumatic tyres. Twelve of these were sent to National, nine in addition to the three already mentioned.

Twenty were fitted with special 22 seat bodies and were painted silver in July 1926 and used on five new routes put on as feeder services from the then newly opened Morden Station on the Northern Line. Gradually all but one of these routes were double decked and the buses transferred to other areas. Seventy five of these single deckers retained their solid tyres due to the fact that they were used on routes having steep hills and so these buses were fitted with Sprag gears. Fifty of the buses in question had only 20 seats and were worked from Muswell Hill garage on route 41 and 111 (the latter now W7). At that time only twenty seater buses could be used on these routes due to weight restrictions over railway bridges. The other solid tyred single deckers had 24 seats and were supplied for two North London and one South London hilly routes namely the 104 (now 240), the 110 (now 210) and the 99 route in the south. A further delivery of eleven K type single deckers in 1928 completed the total of one hundred and forty that were used by General. These though to a similar design had a somewhat larger body to seat 30 passengers and were all used at first on routes in the Kingston and Hounslow areas. By 1928 four of the pneumatic tyred single deckers were transferred to East Surrey and used on routes in the Leatherhead and Guildford districts. By 1925 many of the double deck bodies which had been built in 1920/1 were needing replacement and so some one hundred new K type bodies were built later that year. Another hundred or so bodies were extensively rebuilt. These new or rebuilt bodies could be recognised as they had the "turn under" or curved type of body as used on the NS type. They also had what I would describe as "NS type seating" in the lower deck, these had upholstered backs to the seats whereas the original K type had wooden seat backs. Another difference was glass windows in the upper part of the front bulkhead instead of wooden panels. About fifty of these new or reconditioned bodies had longitudinal seating inside which reduced the seating to 44 passengers. I remember travelling on several of these strange buses at the time but I never knew the reason for the innovation as the buses were scattered through the fleet just a few at certain garages. The twenty five new chassis ordered for the second batch of single deckers were delivered in September and October 1926 and were mounted with double deck bodies. Many of them had the newly built 44 seat bodies. These buses which were numbered K1102-1126 had registrations in the YP and YR series. They were sent to several garages then operating K type vehicles, some having only one, others two or more of these new buses. I remember seeing K1110 on route 80 from Sutton garage, K1111 and 1115 on the 16's from Cricklewood, K1119 on the 53 route and K1108 and 1124 from Nunhead on route 112B (now part of 12). At the same time that these new double deckers were being put into service another six were added to the fleet and these were given numbers K1127-1132, and they had Devon registrations, TA 1004-6, TA 1168-70. They were second hand acquired from Devon General who had taken over the six originally purchased in 1920 by Torquay Tramways Company.

B794 on route 38A and K574 on route 29 working from Palmers Green (AD) garage, where it was delivered new on 19 October 1921 moving to Old Kent Road (P) garage in November 1929, before being withdrawn to Sutton (A) garage in August 1930 and sold to Cohen in December that year.

Early in 1926, certain K type buses appeared in London in new colours. At this time the LGOC had been acquiring many of the Independent bus companies which had been coming on to the London streets since 1922, and continued to work these Dennis, Leyland or Straker Squires buses on their respective routes and under their individual names and livery. During 1926/7 many of these buses were replaced by K type vehicles transferred from the General fleet. Amongst the first of these K type buses in strange livery was Cambrian who had the largest number of these transfers. There were some thirty of them by 1927 and they were painted light green with "Cambrian" fleet name on the sides. They all carried (CA) garage plates but in fact they worked out of General's Hanwell garage, mainly on routes 185, Southall and Liverpool St. and 291, Hounslow Heath and Liverpool St. Then there were three Ks in Shamrock "blue" working on route 14. Four more in Central colours, also seven Royal Blue and four Westerns which worked jointly on route 247, Kings Cross and Greenford. Gradually other K type buses appeared in Independent colours which included RA, Olympic, Ubique, Horseshoe and Primrose. In November 1926 there was a change of plan regarding these acquired independent buses as although the individual companies were continued the vehicles were painted in "General red" and with General fleet name on the side and the only sign that they were allocated to these other companies were the small words on the lower panels showing official ownership. Thus only the interested bus enthusiasts could spot them. All the earlier acquisitions were painted except for Cambrian and the following other companies had their buses replaced by K type from the General fleet all of course being double deck. The acquired companies were Edward Paul, Fleet, Clarence, A1, Lonsdale, Direct, Criterian , Celtic, Imperial, Superbus, Marathon, Florence, Grafton, Legion, Jockey, Alberta, Wellington, Tower, Empress, Invicta, Brittania, Atlas, East Ham, Grangewood, Vivid, Tottenham Hotspur, Cosgrove, White Star, Cambrian Landray, Victoria Road Car, PC and Orange. These are given in the order of acquisition and the last company to have K type replacements was Cambrian which had two single deck K's. These K type buses all continued to work on the routes as worked by the independent companies but operated from LGOC garages except that twenty five K type were grouped to run out of the former Invicta garage at East Ham which was given code E and Batten's garage at East Ham which was given code EH. These buses were Atlas, East Ham, Invicta, Britannia and they worked on the 15 and 23 routes.

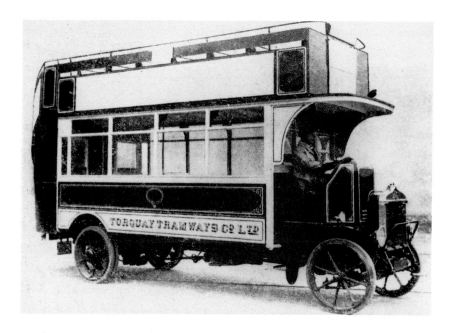

One of six K type buses bought by Torquay Tramways Co. Ltd. in 1920 to operate feeder services to the tramway network. They passed to Devon General who sold them to LGOC in August and September 1926, and were allotted fleet numbers K1127 – 1132 inclusive.

These independent buses only had a short existence as following another change of plan all the independent companies were wound up on 1st January 1928 and their vehicles absorbed by the General and so these K type came back once more to the main fleet.

Early in 1929, East Surrey purchased from United Automobile Services Ltd, two second-hand K type chassis which United had acquired with the business of Robinson's of Scarborough on 1st March 1926, which had previously been registered XB 9084 and AJ 7587. A spare body was also obtained and the result was a new bus produced from all these spare parts but with the important difference that it was fitted with a six-cylinder engine, the only one ever to be used in a K type bus. It was registered PG 1509 with fleet number 66 and operated on route 21 commencing on 1st July 1929. It was withdrawn in May 1930 and scrapped.

K1 (LU8231) seen when it first entered service on route 11 from Hammersmith (R) garage in August 1919. Note the driver's hand signal as he pulls away from the stop.

The K type bus then continued in service in London without much change until early in 1930. By that time the LT and ST type buses were appearing in London and their advent caused the withdrawal of the K type during 1930 and early 1931 except for a few which continued until 1932. By the beginning of October 1930 the double deck K type fleet was reduced to some four hundred and fifty in service. These included the one hundred and sixty two Metropolitan K's all of which continued in use until they were replaced by a similar number of ST type buses between January and March 1931. Two central area routes still had K type buses until replaced by newer vehicles in December 1930, these were 2C, Golders Green and West Norwood and 3B, Camden Town – Crystal Palace. These were from Norwood (N) garage. The General fleet of K type buses was reduced to forty four in service during the first three months of 1931. Thirty nine of these were at Elmers End garage and were used on routes 54 and 494 (later 194). (These routes ran over a weak railway bridge in Addiscombe Road and only K type buses could be used). The other five were at Hounslow for working route 90, Richmond and Chertsey. There were special weight restrictions in connection with Chertsey Bridge and the K type were the only double deckers which could be used on this route so ten continued in service after all others were withdrawn. Ten were needed as the 90 required five buses on weekdays and ten on Sundays. The ten buses were K424, 632, 700, 746, 825, 888, 924, 949, 969 and 1121. These were finally withdrawn from service on 22 June 1932 when route 90 was diverted to Staines and changed to NS type vehicles and a new single deck route put on to serve Chertsey over the bridge. Most though not all of the ten buses retained for the 90 route had the 1925 new or rebuilt bodies including some with the 44 seat longitudinal seating.

During 1930 and 1931 the single deck K's were also withdrawn from service being replaced first by the T type and later by the LT single deckers. The last thirty four were taken out of service in August 1931.

K196 is seen here at a later stage in its life now working from Batten's East Ham Tilbury Road (EH) garage to where it was transferred in January 1928. It is operating duty 14 on route 15A East Ham (White Horse) to Ladbroke Grove (Eagle). (London Transport U5589)

A number of physical changes took place with the K type vehicles during the years in service. When the K type first entered service they were painted red but with the lower panels in chocolate brown but this subsequently changed to an "all red livery". As built all K type buses were fitted with small route number stencils both at the front on the drivers cab roof and at the rear. These were the same size as on the B type vehicles. However, when the S type bus was developed in 1921 a new larger style stencil plate was introduced, and this size was also fitted to all NS type vehicles. After the B type buses were withdrawn from service in 1926 the K type buses were fitted with this larger style of stencil both front and back and this became a standard fitting for all buses then in use. The single deckers had small stencils for the route numbers at the top of the side windows in the front bulkhead. Instead of route or destination boards they were fitted with roller blinds at the front only. Both single and double deck K type buses had a feature unique to the type in carrying their front lamps suspended from the roof of the drivers cab. This idea was not continued with the S or any subsequent type of bus. In August 1922, K191 was fitted with a windscreen in the front of the top deck consisting of five panes 16½ inches high. It ran on route 13 from Hendon (AE) garage. It is reported that twelve other buses had this experimental windscreen namely K453, 470, 518, 608, 636, 754, 763, 766, 849, 850, 954 and 970. K470 went to Cricklewood garage no doubt for route 16 and K954 to Willesden garage for route 6 but the routes and garages of all others are not known.

These fittings seem to have been taken off after quite a short time. Some time during 1924 all K and S type buses were fitted with a triangular board which was suspended from the cab roof in between the headlamps. This board could be turned at will to show any of three faces. One would be blank another to indicate places of interest on the route such as "To and from Olympia". The third side was shown during the hours of 10 am and 4 pm whilst cheap midday fares were in operation and this read "CHEAP MID DAY 1d & 2d FARES BY THIS BUS". These fixtures seem to have been taken off about 1929.

I have no record of any K type bus being used by other operators after withdrawal from London service although two of the 22 seater single deckers were used for a time as Park buses by Whipsnade Zoo.

One bus, K312 was used for a time as the bus for the famous skid patch at Chiswick Works.

Many of the double deckers were sold to George Cohen Sons & Co. Ltd., of Commercial Road, E14 who advertised them for sale on the following terms, "To drive away fully equipped as a bus for £40. Complete body with windows intact free on buyer's vehicle at Fulham depot for £5. Or delivered by road within 25 miles of depot or rail within 200 miles of London for £11." They described the bus bodies as follows. "London bus bodies in perfect condition with all windows intact – some practically new, weatherproof, wired throughout for electric light with standard fittings which can be connected to any existing supply from house or factory, splendid for sports pavilions, summer houses, bathing huts, shelters, etc." This is no doubt the reason why a number of K type bodies have been found rotting away in gardens, allotments etc.

K1090 was delivered new to Kingston (K) garage on 20 November 1925 transferring to Hounslow (AV) garage on 31 March 1926 and on to Slough (Langley Road) (SL) garage when it opened on 8 September 1926. It is seen here working a short journey from Langley to Old Windsor on route 81.

K1060 (XD 8307) in use by Bertram Mills Circus.

Notwithstanding these disposals, it is fortunate that two K type buses have remained intact and in good condition so that we can easily be reminded of these interesting vehicles which were last in service in London well over sixty years ago. The first of these is K424 one of the six former LGOC buses to be seen at the Museum of London Transport Covent Garden. This bus which has registration number KC 8059 is in good working order and is often to be seen outside the Museum on rallies etc. It has often taken part in the annual London to Brighton run of Historic Commercial Vehicles. In fact K424 has been on many of these runs arranged by the Historic Commercial Vehicle Club which was formed in 1958. This run is quite a feat for a vehicle of this age and size and its participation creates considerable interest. I was able to travel home from Brighton on the top deck of K424 on the rally held on Sunday, 2nd May 1965. The journey brought back many memories of travelling on this type of bus in years past. In spite of the solid tyres, travelling was remarkably smooth due to the speed which could seldom exceed 20 mph. I was reminded of the familiar jerk when starting which always occurred with this type of bus. Travelling inside I also remembered the somewhat unique "phit phit" sound of the engine.

K1053 was one of a few single deckers acquired by the Safety Coach Service in Jersey and re-registered J 5672. They were all fitted with homemade windscreens as these were not permitted in London.

There was some doubt whether the bus would be ready for the 1965 run due to a cracked crankcase but AEC came to the rescue and had completed the repairs in time for the bus to have some preliminary trips prior to the long run to Brighton. The K completed the journey very well and carried some VIPs in the persons of the Mayor and Mayoress of Lambeth who were joined at the Brighton boundary by the Mayor and Mayoress of Brighton. The return journey meant climbing several hills and a stop for water was necessary on the way. The following year the HCVC Brighton run took place on Sunday 1st May and my wife and I were privileged to take part and invited to travel on the top deck of K424 for the complete trip there and back, a most interesting experience.

It will be remembered that K424 was one of the ten buses retained at Hounslow for route 90 and was in service until June 1932. It has one of the new 1925 bodies or maybe one that was rebuilt at that time, as it has the curved body and the later NS type seating.

One more K type bus has been preserved namely K502 which has the registration number XC 8117. It was among a batch of K type sold off about 1930 through George Cohen for use as a hen house on an egg farm and later converted to living accommodation for a farm worker. It was rescued by Barry Weatherhead in 1968 who spent many hours, over 20,000 in fact in research and restoration to bring this bus as close to its original state as possible. It had one of the Short Bros bodies that had been rebuilt with the `turn under' sides. It has been given the route boards for the 53 route, West Hampstead and Plumstead Common and running number P11 as it had once been allocated to Old Kent Road garage for this route. It has taken part in most of the London to Brighton rallies since 1975.

K364 joined the "Metropolitan" fleet at Chelverton Road Putney (AF) garage on 8 April 1925 and stayed there until sold to Cohens in February 1931. It is seen here caught in traffic near Marble Arch on route 74B Camden Town to Putney High Street Station.

THE LONDON
S TYPE MOTOR BUS

The K type first introduced in 1919 soon became a most useful bus and over a hundred were in service by June 1920. The increased capacity of the 46-seat K over that of the B type restricted to 34 seats was most acceptable but the LGOC soon realised that a still larger bus was necessary, therefore in April 1920 a 56-seat body was built. For this body numbered 5217 the AEC provided an experimental chassis number 21004. It had K type wheels and to partly offset the increased length of the body the bonnet protruded beyond the front wheels. It does not seem to have gone on trial although a photograph shows it had bonnet number T1 and a side route number 123. This chassis was not owned by the LGOC so it was sold by the AEC to Hubert Green of Wells with a lorry body and registered PW 8649.

However after the maximum laden weight for a double decker had been increased to 8 tons a larger bus was put in hand. The AEC designed a new chassis with a larger engine increased to 35 hp 108 mm bore x 140 mm stroke and it had larger wheels. A new body was built by the LGOC and this, body number 5257, was ready on 14 September 1920. It had 57 seats, 29 passengers inside and 28 on the top deck. Inside it had five rows of transverse seats and a seat for five against the front panel facing backwards and longitudinal seats for four over the rear wheels. It had larger size route number stencil boxes front and back and also on each side in the centre of the windows. When it made its trial trip in London in November 1920 it had route number 123 but route boards for the 11 service, Shepherds Bush and Liverpool Street. There must have been some problem with the backward facing seats as after it was submitted for police approval on 10th December it had become a 54-seater only 26 inside and the longitudinal seats at the doorway being six on each side.

S1 was the first of the 54 seaters built in September 1920 and although it is shown here in "General" livery with route 123 in a posed photograph for the press, it spent its working life in the "Metropolitan" fleet, seeing service at Hammersmith (R), Turnham Green (V), Putney Bridge (F), Camberwell (Q), Tottenham (AR) and Chelverton Road, Putney (AF) garages before withdrawal in July 1931. (C F Klapper)

This new bus with bonnet number S1 and registration number XC 8183 went into service on 29 December 1920 working from Turnham Green (V) garage on route 17 Ealing and London Bridge together with K type buses. It stayed on the 17 route until 18th January 1921 when a second S type was ready and this was S10 and both went to Hammersmith (R) garage for route 11. S10 with registration XC 8266 appears to have had body 5217 altered from 56 seats to 54.

It was decided to build and test the first fifteen S type to ascertain how the larger buses worked out in service. During February 1921 twelve more S type had been built and were sent to Hammersmith garage and eight were soon working on the 11 route. Others were tried out on two other routes two being put on to 32, Shepherds Bush and Wimbledon Common and two on the 88, Acton Green and Mitcham also from R garage. This lasted until 23 March 1921 when all fifteen S type were sent to Turnham Green garage and operated on the 88 service.

These buses proving very satisfactory in service an order for another two hundred and fifty S type chassis was placed with AEC. Two hundred bodies for these buses were built by the LGOC at their North Road body works and the other fifty by Dodson. The first bus of this order S17 arrived on 1 July and this was sent to Merton (AL) garage for route 88. Another twenty buses were sent to AL garage to cover the allocation of ten for the 88 and also eleven for the 32 route. Twenty more S type went to Hammersmith (R) which also ran on the 32 and 88. During October 1921 S type returned to the important 11 service with fifty buses to R garage and another fifty to Dalston (D). During the same month with over one hundred and fifty S type being in service twenty six went to Palmers Green (AD) being part of the allocation for the 29 Victoria Station and Southgate. Up to this time all the S type buses had replaced or joined routes worked by K type but there was a change with the next route that had S type late in October and during November. This was the 16 Victoria and Cricklewood working from Cricklewood (W) garage as twenty eight S type operated with the smaller B type. During November and December some twenty buses went to Leyton (T) for route 10A Elephant and Epping Town. Later a few more went to Cricklewood for the 16 and eventually S264 arrived on 2 February on that service.

S569 of the "Metropolitan" fleet is seen taking layover at Morden Station Underground before starting a journey to Walton on the Hill on route 165, probably between May 1930 and January 1931 when it was at Sutton (A) garage for the second time in its working life. (Noel Jackson)

It is recorded that in May 1922 that some modification had to be made to the original fifteen S type to convert the chassis to standard S type.

S237 of Sutton (A) garage is seen outside the All England Tennis Ground at Wimbledon doing a turn on route 190 Wimbledon Station to Southfields Station via Merton Road. (Noel Jackson)

A further three hundred and seventy five S type chassis were supplied by the AEC during 1922 and so orders for the double deck bodies required were placed with Dodson and Short Brothers. These new buses began to arrive early in July 1922 with eight going to Cricklewood garage to complete the allocation for the 16 route. An interesting point arises in connection with them as during a visit to town that July I remember walking up Park Lane noting the numbers of the 16 route buses which were in the S200s when I saw three new ones S642, 643 and 644 and I was surprised at seeing these so much out of sequence. Much later I found that these three chassis had been built up at Chiswick Works and not supplied by AEC and that they had been sent to Cricklewood garage on 3 July 1922 just before S268 and 269. S type that continued to enter service in July and August went to various garages Merton (AL) and Forest Gate (G). Then in August a number went to Holloway (J) and to Putney (F) for the 14 route Hornsey Rise & Putney. September saw the S type being put on to the 12 route Shepherds Bush and Dulwich working from Nunhead (AH) garage. In October it was the turn of the 15 service (Ladbroke Grove and East Ham) to get the S type which came from Middle Row (X) and Forest Gate (G) garages. By December there were some six hundred and forty S type in use in London.

In March 1922 the LGOC had built at the Farm Lane works a prototype single deck body to seat 32 and this was mounted on S265. It was sent to Kingston (K) garage on 3 April and tried out on the 115 Kingston – Guildford route and other single deck routes in the area. This bus proving successful the LGOC built another thirty-four similar single deckers but these however were 30 seaters. They entered service on a number of routes during September and October 1922. On 6 September five single deck buses S369, 371, 377, 382 and 384 went to Acton (E) garage for the short 55 route Acton and Grove Park, Chiswick. They continued until April 1924 when they were replaced by open top NS type. Seven single decks S303, 331, 354, 387, 388, 389, 390 were transferred to the National Omnibus & Transport Company at Watford where they were operated on behalf of the LGOC. These all had NK registration numbers but two others which also went to National were S265, the prototype and S9 an early bus in for overhaul whose double deck body was replaced by a new single deck one. National ran these buses on the N13 service Watford to Barnet and Enfield later numbered 306. One more single deck was sent to National in October this was S327 which had a 30-seat experimental one man body. It is not known what routes it was tried out on but in December it was sent to Reigate for trial by the East Surrey until in May 1923 it was sent back to the LGOC. The OMO body was taken off and sold to the AEC and S327 was given a standard S type body and sent to Kingston garage in June 1923. This bus with its NK 4473 registration number spent the rest of its time with the LGOC. Nine single decks were sent to

Athol Street (C) in September for the 108 route Poplar and Greenwich through the Blackwall Tunnel. They replaced B type single deckers during September and October 1922 however on 29 November these nine buses were transferred to Dalston (D) garage to assist in the operation of a new service, 108A Clapton and Lewisham and so B type were put back on to the 108 and also on part of the 108A. Three buses, S433, 439 and 442 went to Streatham (AK) to replace B type on the 87 route Streatham Common and Purley. This left seven single deck S type to go to Kingston (K) for two routes, 79 Kingston and Woking and 113 Kingston and Sutton.

...00 on route 13 Golders Green Station Underground to London Bridge Station, during the general strike in ...ay 1926. Note the police constable sitting alongside the driver. In this instance Cricklewood (W) garage ...ovided 65 buses, the usual allocation being Cricklewood (W) 26 and Hendon (AE) 24. The crew were ...unteers and the fares limited to 3d.

A view of S814 on route 25 working from Seven Kings (AP) garage, where it resided from March 1923 to 1927.

The final delivery of S type chassis from the AEC covering numbers from S645 to 895 arrived during 1923. Short Brothers supplied 150 double deck bodies and forty from Ransomes others being built by LGOC. These bodies were built with the 'turn under' side panels that is they were curved like the NS not straight as the earlier models. During subsequent overhauls the two styles of body were intermixed and the 'turn under' bodies found their way on many of the earlier S type. Sixteen new S type were put into service in January 1923, about twenty in February whilst in March a total of 138 were licensed for use, and thirty arrived in April. Many of these buses went to Palmers Green (AD) for the 29 route, others to Seven Kings (AP) for the 25 and Tottenham (AR) for the 76. Meanwhile the LGOC was proceeding with the new NS type of bus and the first twenty five had come into service early in May. Nevertheless, there were twelve S type ready to be placed and seven were sent to Old Kent Road (P) in May two others in July then the last three S883, 894 and 895 were sent to the new though small Loughton (L) garage on 3 August for route 10B Elephant and Epping Town. By this time most of the main bus routes such as 3, 9, 10, 11, 12, 14, 15, 19, 25, 29 were operated by S type but the 16 had reverted to K type.

The remaining twenty-nine AEC S type chassis were scheduled for a further batch of single deck buses and between March and July 1923 the LGOC built 30-seat saloon bodies for them. Apart from S776 and 780 all were numbered in the S800s. Fifteen of them went to Athol Street (C) to replace the B type still working on the Blackwall Tunnel routes 108 and 108A, and in October 1923 the 108A was extended from Lewisham to Forest Hill. S835 and 841 were sent to East Surrey Traction Company for use on the S3 service West Croydon and Sevenoaks which later became the 403. The two buses were sent back to the LGOC in April 1925 and I saw them working on the 108A and was surprised to see they had Surrey registrations PD 5981 and 5983. Four more went to National at Watford these were S839, 855, 859, 865. In August four buses S780, 858, 866 and 875 were put on the 87 route working from Streatham (AK). The last three S776, 877 and 881 together with S327 returned from East Surrey went to Kingston (K) in August 1923 for the 115 route to Guildford.

S144 had been in use as an experimental lorry at Chiswick since September 1921 but in November 1923 its lorry body was removed and replaced by a 54 seat double deck body with registration XP 4188 and allocated to Battersea (B) garage.

A Wimbledon scene showing S36 of Merton (AL) garage on route 32 – note the board under the driver's canopy advertising cheap midday fares – followed by K225 (LU 8466) on 39A special service to the Lawn Tennis ground at Wimbledon.

S92 takes layover at Shepherds Bush (S) garage before returning to Liverpool Street on route 11 in the spring of 1921.

A number of additional S type chassis were built up at Chiswick Works for various purposes. First was S896 which was fitted with an experimental lorry body E1 in June 1923 until in June 1924 S896 was given a 29-seat open charabanc body and registered as XR 9985. It had a 'cape cart' hood folded at the back but which could be brought forward over the vehicle in bad weather. This charabanc body was sold in May 1927 and replaced by a 54 seat double deck body and sent to W garage. Three other S type were built up S897, 898 and 899 all 54 seat double deck with registrations XO 9229/30/1. They went to Tottenham (AR) on 3 September 1923. The following built up chassis must have been S900 but nothing is known of it though it is possible that it was a lorry sold complete in 1924 to AEC. S901 was a chassis supplied by the AEC fitted with a 30 seat single deck body and sent to National at Watford in May 1924 having registration NK 7365. S902 was another experimental lorry new early in February 1925 but later that month it too became a double deck bus with registration XU 6193 and sent to Leyton (T). In February 1927 another twelve S type were built by the LGOC these being S903 to 914, all with double deck bodies. Four of them S904, 906 908 and 910 were sent to National for the Romford service 308, that ran from Stapleford Abbots to Aveley. In May 1928 this route was taken over by the LGOC so the four National buses were sent to Ware garage for the 310 Hertford and Enfield Town. The eight General S type went to Cricklewood (W) garage. Another thirteen S type single deckers were added to the National fleet in February 1927 and were numbered S915 – 927 and registered by the LGOC as YH 1101 – 1113. These buses had an improved style of body similar to the K type single deck with the route numbers at the top of the rounded corners of the front bulkhead. They were allocated to Watford for routes 306 and 311.

An interior view of the lower deck of S1 – note the wooden backs to the seats.
(London Transport U108)

S928 was the last of the type built by the LGOC and it was first used as a ticket van being sent to the Ticket Department on 18 November 1927, it had registration YT 4898.

During January 1923 a start was made in transferring to the fleet of Tramways (MET) Omnibus Company a number of S type buses and these were repainted with the fleet name METROPOLITAN instead of General. Replacement of the original MET fleet of B type had commenced a few months earlier with the transfer of K type and by June 1923 the MET fleet consisted of one hundred and thirty three K type and seventy seven S type . The latter came within two batches S1 to S63 and S216 to S284. At first these seventy seven buses were found at many garages and on various routes but after the London Traffic Act came into force on 1 December 1924 the seventy seven S type buses were allocated to four garages Camberwell (Q), Tottenham (AR), Sutton (A) and Hammersmith (R) in order to work on the 69 and 88 group of routes. The allocations were:

Route 69	Wormley – Camberwell Green	Q10, AR11
Route 88	Acton Green – Belmont	A21
Route 88A	Acton Green – Mitcham	R18
Route 88B	Oxford Circus – Mitcham	A11

From 17 February 1926 the Sutton allocations on routes 88 and 88B were transferred to Merton (AL) garage. Spare MET buses were kept at each garage so only MET buses ran on the specified routes. Route 88A was changed on 7 December 1927 as route 288, when it ran to Grove Park, Chiswick instead of Acton Green and ran under a low bridge unsuitable for an S type bus so twenty one NS type were transferred to MET and the same number of the S type returned to the LGOC. One S type bus S70 was transferred to the South Metropolitan Tramways Company with nine K type in August 1923. This company had the fleet name of SOUTHERN. One extra S type bus S569 was passed to the MET in November 1924.

One of the provisions of the 1924 Traffic Act was that all variations or short workings of route should have a separate number or a suffix letter so when this came into force on 1 December use of the illuminated route numbers on the sides of the S type was discontinued and instead route numbers were shown on wooden boards in the centre of each side of the top deck as on the K type.

S920 was one of the last batch of single deckers allocated to National in the summer of 1927. It is seen in LGOC days at Potters Bar on route 313 St. Albans to Enfield (George). (J F Higham)

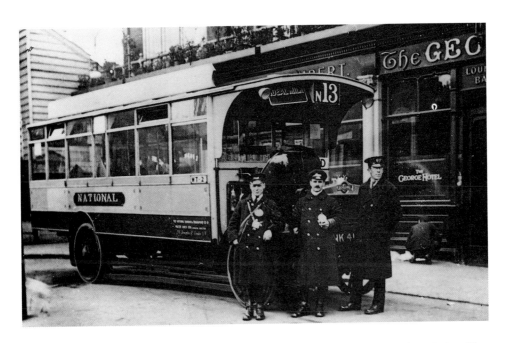

This could be S303 (NK4115), S331 (NK 4189) or S354 (NK 4188) allocated to the "National" Watford Leavesden Road (WT) garage in July and August 1922. It is seen at The George, Enfield awaiting departure to Watford on route N13.

It was in March 1922 that the AEC began to make the S type available to other operators the bus being known as the 403 model and this number was added to the chassis number. All AEC chassis for the LGOC were numbered on from 20001 for K1 and it had reached 21005 for S1. The first sales were 403001 – 403002 to Robinsons of Scarborough two single decks AJ 7782 and AJ 8492. In August 1922 the East Surrey Traction Company obtained six 403 type. They were 403015 – 403020 and they had 48 seat double deck bodies by Shorts and were registered PC 9317-22 and East Surrey fleet numbers 91 to 96.

Some of the National routes needed larger buses so the LGOC introduced the PS class considered as the 'Provincial S type'. They were AEC 502 model having the more powerful S-type 6.8 litre engine and early in 1923 the LGOC ordered twelve 502 chassis from AEC for National. Double deck bodies seating 43 were built by the LGOC and the first three PS1 – 3 were sent to Watford on 5 May 1923. The LGOC had however obtained an earlier chassis 403074 for which they built a 54-seat double deck body with the registration XN 1800. It was sent to Hammersmith (R) garage and operated on route 11 from 8 January 1923. This lasted until 18 May when it was sent to National as PS4. Between 29 June and 18 July, PS5 to PS13 were licensed for service. These PS type ran on route N1, St Albans and Rickmansworth and N6, Watford and Berkhamstead also on N14 St Albans and Hemel Hempstead. Between May and July 1927 the seating on these PS buses was increased from 43 to 54.

In 1924 it was the turn of the East Surrey to have new buses which were provided by the LGOC for East Surrey to operate. Thirty of the 502 model were ordered from AEC and for these Ransomes built 48 seat double deck bodies of a type unique to East Surrey. They had a body similar to the NS with the white curved canopy over the driver but being higher from the ground needing three steps for passengers to board thus identical to S type. They were delivered between 24 May and 4 July1924 with registrations PD 9752 to 9756 and PD 1348 to 1372. At first all were the property of the LGOC but on 15 July twelve of them were sold to East Surrey for their own routes. They were useful in working some hilly routes S6 Kingston and Redhill, the long S9 West Croydon, East Grinstead and Uckfield, S10 Bromley – Reigate and East Surrey's S24 Reigate and Sevenoaks. Although considered as a PS type these letters were not used instead East Surrey fleet numbers 112 to 132/134-142 was shown on the bonnet. During January 1926 another six 502 type were supplied to East Surrey but these had the standard S type body built by the LGOC with registrations PE 8309-14 and East Surrey fleet numbers 143-8. They were allocated to Godstone garage for routes 409 and 410 formerly S9 and S10. At the same time two similar buses were built for National being numbered PS14 and 15 with registrations RO 2974/5 they were the last of the 502 model chassis. Another eight PS type were delivered to East Surrey in March 1927. They were the improved 507 model and had 48 seat bodies by LGOC to the East Surrey style with the curved white canopy over the driver. They had East Surrey fleet numbers 168-175 and registrations PF 9016-23. The eight were allocated to Reigate garage for route 406 as their larger engines provided more power to cope with the steep gradient of Reigate Hill.

S327 had a varied life. It entered service with "National" in October 1922 transferring to East Surrey in the December. By June 1923 it was back with LGOC and served at Kingston (K), Dalston (D), Sutton (A) and Hounslow (AV) garages, before being withdrawn in November 1932. It was relicensed in May 1933 serving at Nunhead (AH) and Elmers End (ED) garages before arriving at Enfield (E) garage on 16 May 1934 where it remained until withdrawn in April 1936. Note the Hertfordshire registration NK4473 and the ADC radiator. It is seen here in service on route 242 (whose basic route was Waltham Cross (Eleanor Cross Road) to Waltham Abbey (Green Man)) working on the Tuesday, Thursday and Saturday extension to Epping Forest (Volunteer). (J F Higham)

It has already been mentioned that the AEC had made the S type chassis available to other operators in 1922. Those for outside sales were known as the 403 model a total of one hundred and thirty eight being provided which went to many bus operators throughout the country having either 54 seat double deck bodies or as single decks. Among the first of the 403 double decks were two for Manchester Corporation and ten for South Wales Transport. Whilst the LGOC had all fifty of the 502 model for East Surrey and National it was the similar 503 model that featured in the outside sales list and one hundred and forty eight were built. The first fifteen 503s in March 1922 went to Birmingham City Transport. South Wales also had thirty five as double deck as well as two charabancs. The 504 model introduced in 1924 had a slightly lowered frame which enabled Birmingham City Transport to fit a covered top deck to it. The initial bus which had registration OL 8100 and new in July 1924 was the first motor bus to go into service in this country with a covered top deck. It was so successful that Birmingham Transport had one hundred and seven more of the 504 model all with covered tops. Birmingham City Transport also had one hundred and twenty five of the later 507 model between 1927 and 1929 and these had pneumatic tyres. Thirty five of them had specially built low height bodies as they ran on a route which passed under two low bridges. On the top deck they had bucket seats similar to the tunnel type NS in London. A total of two hundred and thirty eight of the 507 model were built by AEC between March 1926 and March 1929 being sold to many bus operators. It will be seen that in Birmingham the S type of bus had covered tops, pneumatic tyres and the 507 even had enclosed driver's cabs none of which were permitted in London for the S type.

The double deck S type buses in London continued to give good service although by 1925 the new NS double decks had replaced them on many of the main Central London bus routes with the result that many S type were transferred to other garages and operated on a number of suburban routes. By February 1927 the average number of S type double decks scheduled for service on weekdays was 700 and these were allocated to twenty-one garages. The garages with most S type were Leyton (T) with one hundred and thirty six buses on seven routes, Merton (AL) sixty five buses on five routes and Camberwell (Q) sixty four buses on three routes. S type were sent to some of the smaller suburban garages such as Edgware (EW) twenty three buses for routes 142, 158 and 307A, South Harrow (SH) six for the 114 route. Romford (RD) ten for 66 and 86 routes. A similar average number of scheduled S type buses continued in use until the end of 1930. But by then the new ST and LT type of bus was being delivered in quantity and began to take over from the S type so fifty were withdrawn in January 1931. At the end of March 1931 only five hundred and fourteen double deck S type were scheduled for service and by 5 August this number was reduced to two hundred and sixty five. Eventually during November 1931 the last sixty S type double decks were withdrawn from service.

S391 transferred from Merton (AL) garage to Harrow Weald (HD) garage in April 1930 is seen standing at the Red Lion Pinner, before returning to North Harrow Station on route 353. (C F Klapper)

The country area PS type had already started to disappear as in May 1930 new ST type buses had been sent to the National at Watford to replace the fifteen PS type buses on the N1 and N6 routes. Nine standard STs ran on the N1 but six low bridge ST types were built for the N6 later to be numbered 336.

S836 transferred from Dalston (D) garage to Harrow Weald (HD) on 9 April 1930, the day it opened, is now equipped with pneumatic tyres. It is working on route 219 inaugurated on 10 June 1931 between North Wembley (near Preston Road Station) to Wembley (Ealing Road). Note the enhancing white background to the route number in the blind box. (C F Klapper)

It was in 1931 that East Surrey had STs to replace their PS type and the LGOC supplied thirty of the new vehicles between March and June and they enabled the PSs to be taken off the 403 and 409 routes, the 406 having had some new buses earlier. However the low bridge at Godstone on the 410 route prevented normal height buses being used and pending the delivery of special vehicles eleven of the PS type were retained for service on this route. They consisted of eight of the first batch of PS namely PD 9754/5/6, PD 1355/58/59/63/68, two of the 1926 delivery PE 8309/10 and one 507 model PE 9018. East Surrey's six S type PC 9317-22 had remained in use and ran at times on the 410 route. All seventeen of these early buses passed to London General Country Services in 1932 and later to London Transport. Following the delivery of the twelve new low bridge STLs in May 1934 all PS and S type were withdrawn.

The fourteen single deck type National buses were withdrawn

from service in June 1929 and sold. They were replaced on the 306 route by the new Reliance R type single decks. The later single deck Nationals S915-927 continued in service so they passed to London General Country Services in 1932 and in due course to London Transport being withdrawn by early 1935.

S371 awaits departure at Windsor Castle on route 503 to Uxbridge in 1932, after being equipped with a closed driver's cab. This was an Uxbridge (UX) garage working although the vehicle was officially allocated to Hounslow (AV) garage, the parents' shed. (J F Higham)

Reverting to LGOC central area operations it is to be noted that there was little change with the fifty S type single deckers and they continued much the same until on 19 October 1927 when the special tunnel type NS buses were introduced for working through Blackwall Tunnel. The 108 route was then divided into two sections the NS buses ran as 108B Poplar and Forest Hill whilst the northern part of the route between Clapton and Poplar ran as 108D and due to some low bridges still needed single deck buses. The ten S type that had been on the 108 were moved to other garages. During 1928 all these single deck buses were fitted with pneumatic tyres with a great saving in the annual road Tax which was reduced from £72 to £57.12.0. Thus fitted with pneumatics the S type continued to give good service for another three years being used on a number of different single deck routes. But new single deck buses were being introduced the T type in 1930 followed by the single deck LT class and gradually during 1931 they replaced the S type. This commenced in May when new LTs were sent to Dalston (D) for the 108D, and by the 7 October 1931 only seven S type single decks were scheduled for operation. Three of them were working from Enfield (E) garage on the 306B/F route Waltham Cross and Waltham Abbey or journeys to Epping Forest. The other four were at Uxbridge (UX) garage for routes 501 and 503 Uxbridge and Hounslow or Windsor.

Many S type were re-licensed for further use and during 1932 those in service were fitted with glass windscreens. On 30 May 1933 some sixteen of them were brought back into use during the summer months as extra buses at weekends Saturdays and Sundays, five were sent to Elmers End (ED) and three to Nunhead (AH) all these were required for the 109 route Penge and Chislehurst. Five went to Kingston (K) and three to Hounslow (AV) for their local routes. All these buses became the property of the LPTB on 1st July 1933 and so the fleet name on these S type was changed from GENERAL to LONDON TRANSPORT.

As there was a shortage of suitable single deckers London Transport made use of the S type when introducing new routes. The 230 service Northwick Park and North Harrow had commenced on 1 January 1933 with small OMO Darts but later needed larger buses so eight S type were re-licensed and sent to Harrow Weald (HD) garage on 16 May 1934. The eight were S377, 386, 425, 447, 512, 531, 890, 892. At the same time the four S type on 501 and 503 routes were replaced by T type, but Enfield (E) still had S327, 424, 442 and 458 for the 306 route which on 3 October 1934 was renumbered as 242.

Another short new route commenced on 4 June 1935 the 235 which ran from South Croydon to Selsdon and for this four buses S369, 371, 873 and 887 were sent to Croydon (TC) garage. This did not last long as on 25 March 1936 T type were put on the 235 and the S type withdrawn. The 242 had new buses on the 8 April and Enfield's four S type were withdrawn. The eight working from Harrow Weald garage on the 230 route were actually the last S type in service in London and were withdrawn on 17 June 1936 being replaced by Q type.

S433 of Kingston (K) garage appears well clear of the flood water working on route 62
Kingston to Staines during winter floods in the Thames Valley.

The small Omnibus concern of Capitol Omnibuses of Romford suffered
a serious fire on 17 July 1931 and two of its fleet of four buses were
destroyed. In order to continue operation for a time LGOC loaned four
S type S384, 866, 873 and 884 to Capitol from 18 August to 24
November 1931.

In 1928 the LGOC decided to replace its fleet of B type ticket and
catering vans with S type so in May and June 1928 twelve double deck
S type buses were withdrawn from service and fitted with new van
bodies. Nine became Ticket Vans for use in distributing the printed
tickets to the various garages in London daily. The nine were S85, 95,
157, 162, 167, 406, 419, 445, 521. The other three S374, 416 and 436 were
Catering Vans. These vans were fitted with pneumatic tyres in 1929 and
glass windscreens in 1932. S928 had been a Ticket Van since November
1927 but in March 1931 its van body was transferred to S71 which
became another Catering Van. S928 was given a double deck bus body
and it was sent to Battersea (B) garage.

S384 as a single decker worked from Enfield (E) Turnham Green (V) Sutton (A) Kingston (K) and Sidcup (SP) garages before being loaned to the Capitol Transport Co. of Romford, after a garage fire destroyed their own vehicles. It later worked from Hornchurch (RD), Uxbridge (UX) and Elmers End (ED) garages before being withdrawn in May 1934. It was then fitted with a special open top body for tree lopping duties and was sent to Nunhead (AH) garage on 31 December 1934 as 16S of the miscellaneous service vehicle fleet. (W J Haynes)

Four of the Ticket Vans were sold in April 1933. The remainder continued in use by London Transport and in November 1939 they were numbered in the Service Vehicle series as 11S to 15S respectively for Ticket Vans S 85, 162, 419, 445, and 521. The Catering Vans were numbered 18S to 20S. The number 16S was given to S384 which in 1935 had been fitted with a special double deck open top van body for tree lopping and painted green.

Two double deck S type have been preserved thus giving us a good reminder of this type of London bus. The first is S742 one that was retained by London Transport as an example of its type. It had first been registered on 16 April 1923 and allocated to Tottenham (AR) garage for route 76. It was at Sutton (A) when withdrawn from service on 4 November 1931. It has one of the 'turn under' bodies (body number 6783) built by Ransomes in February 1923. Although one of the vehicles owned by London Transport it is now at the National Motor Museum at Beaulieu in Hampshire.

Another dual numbered vehicle loaned S841 of London General became in May 1923 No. 43 of East Surrey; it was returned in April 1925. It is photographed at the Red Deer terminus in South Croydon possibly ready to leave its shortworking to run to Sevenoaks. The route was renumbered 403 in December 1924. (E. G. Masterman)

The other preserved S type is S454 owned by Michael Banfield who had found it and has carefully restored it. S454 was delivered new to Nunhead (AH) garage on 20 October 1922 and it operated for some four years on route 12. The body which has been restored has the number 6120 indicating that it had been built by Dodson in July 1920 and has the earlier straight sided lower panel. It was sold to the War Department on 27 April 1931 and sold again a month later its subsequent history is not known. It was eventually found by Michael Banfield in a breakers yard near Tring in Hertfordshire in June 1965. It was purchased and taken to the garage in Nunhead Lane which was then owned by Charles W. Banfield Ltd., a coach company. This was founded by Charles William Banfield, Michael's father. He had been a bus driver for the LGOC at Nunhead (AH) garage and could well have driven S454 in those days. Sadly he died in 1966 soon after restoration of this bus commenced. Fortunately the bus was mechanically complete but the body needed much rebuilding and this work was helped considerably with the loan of S742 by London Transport and also of the original body drawings. The only difference between the two bodies is that S742 has the rounded lower panel instead of the straight sides of S454. The restoration took two years and S454 was ready to take part in the Historic Commercial Vehicle Club's 1968 London to Brighton run. It was resplendent with the red livery and GENERAL fleet name and route boards for the 12 service Dulwich, The Plough and Shepherds Bush the route to which it had been allocated way back in 1922.

S228 leads a line of deliveries from bodybuilders Dodsons in 1921.

THE STORY OF THE
NS TYPE BUS

The AEC NS type of bus had an active service life in London of just over fourteen years from May 1923 until November 1937. They were fourteen eventful years as far as motor buses are concerned and to London in particular. When the first NS bus appeared all double deck buses were open topped, had solid tyres so were restricted to a speed limit of 12 mph and no drivers were protected by windscreens. When the last NS was withdrawn in the winter of 1937, all London buses had pneumatic tyres and travelled at speeds in excess of 20 mph, all were fitted with windscreens to the driver's cab, all had covered top deck on double deckers. There were many mechanical improvements with the respective types that followed in the wake of the NS and many of them featured first on the NS type as it is interesting to relate.

NS58 is shown in Chiswick Works when new. Note the Metropolitan Stage Carriage number painted to the left of the entrance to the lower deck, and the actual plate fixed to the rear of the platform.

A change of ownership had also occurred during the life of the NS which had been introduced by the London General Omnibus Company at a time of considerable competition but the last one was operated by London Passenger Transport Board which had in the meantime become the sole owners of London's buses and trains.

The early motor bus had one major fault when compared with the majority of the trams which had covered top decks, but all buses had to have open tops due to the height of the platform floor and the ratio between height and width. This made top covers impossible. Therefore as an outcome of the Chief Engineer of LGOC visit to the USA the idea was put forward for a bus with a single step and lower centre of gravity. The result was that the NS type of chassis which was developed jointly by AEC and the LGOC assuming that the lower floor level would enable the fitting of a top deck cover which would be acceptable to the Metropolitan Police. Alas this was not the case and the licensing of a covered top bus in London was delayed for over three years.

It was late in November 1922 that the first NS chassis was completed by the AEC and in the meantime a suitable body had been designed and built by the LGOC. This had a detachable top cover which could be removed in twenty minutes. This vehicle was submitted to tests early in 1923 given registration number XM 2452 and presented to the Metropolitan Police for examination but they would not relax their stringent regulations and allow this covered top bus to work in London, fearing that it would be top heavy. The bus was withdrawn, the registration number taken up by an S type vehicle and when NS1 eventually entered service at a much later date it had another registration number. It was another three years before the Metropolitan Police would permit covered top buses in London. In the meantime, Birmingham had succeeded as the Corporation had produced a top covered bus to a similar style to the LGOC but mounted on the higher AEC 504 type chassis which was the same height as the General S type bus. This bus was 101 in Birmingham's fleet and registered OL 8100, it entered service on 24 July 1921.

Although the Police would not permit the use of an NS with top cover, the LGOC and AEC went ahead with the designing of the NS type of bus and another chassis (NS2) was delivered to the LGOC on 26

January 1923. It was fitted with a lorry body and sent to the Experimental Department at Farm Lane. NS5 soon followed and LGOC built a suitable open topped body. This vehicle having been passed by the Police the production of the NS class in quantity was put in hand in spite of the fact that they all had to enter service as open top vehicles. The LGOC placed an initial order for 850 chassis following it up a few months later by the order of another 500 which shows the faith they had in this new type as well as the urgent need for new buses to replace obsolete vehicles.

Interior view of the lower deck of NS58 – note the inscription over the entrance to the saloon Metropolitan Stage Carriage 7613, and the upholstered seating. (London Transport U1791)

The first order for bodies amounted to eight hundred and sixty being four hundred and fifty from Short Bros of Rochester, one hundred and eighty five from Brush and two hundred and fifteen being built by LGOC themselves at Chiswick Works. The five hundred of the second order were two hundred and fifty from Shorts, one hundred from Ransomes Sims and Jeffries and one hundred and fifty by

General. A further two hundred and fifty chassis were subsequently ordered taking the total up to NS1605. The later body order of two hundred and seventy five including twenty five spares for overhaul being Short Bros. One hundred and seventy five, Brush seveny five and LGOC twenty five. All bodies were to the same design irrespective of builder.

The choice of NS for the type code for this improved design was strange, as up to that time all General buses had been allocated a single code letter. It was suggested that NS indicated "no step", but the LGOC claimed the letters stood for "nulli secundus" as the design was regarded as "second to none". The trade press at the time were most enthusiastic about the new type of bus indicating that the single step from the road to the platform was only 13 inches high which must have seemed wonderful at the time although it has since become quite commonplace and standard for most double deckers; the NS platform was actually 12 inches lower than that of the S type which needed three steps to reach the platform. At 15ft 6 in, the NS wheelbase was six inches longer than the S type wheelbase; and the laden weight was 8 tons 7 cwt., compared with 8 tons 10 cwt. of the S, 7 tons for the K and 6 tons for the B type. The 35 hp water-cooled engine had four cylinders, cast in pairs, of 108 mm bore by 140 mm stroke. The clutch was the multi-disc pattern running in oil, and there was a constant mesh gear box with helical gears; the back axle was of the double reduction type having a work gear in the centre, mounted in the differential and two pinions on the extreme ends of the driving shaft which engaged in two internally toothed drums on the wheels themselves. The constant mesh helical gear box was claimed to be the most silent of any box at the time and it superseded the chain gear which was apt to be noisy. This was the position upon the introduction of the type but after over 300 had entered service NS385 to NS396 were given chain gear boxes which later became standard for subsequent deliveries. Other experiments in gear boxes took place so that with the first 1600 buses some five types of gear box were in use. The large diameter wheel, first introduced with the AEC S type was retained for the NS. The first NS chassis – 22150 – although built late in 1922 did not enter service until July 1923 when it had registration number XO 1019. Its original body minus its detachable top eventually was used for a later NS bus. Its top deck rail was different to the usual standard and it never actually had a top cover in service. The earliest registration number given to an NS – XN 1745 – was to be found on NS25 and by May 1923 when the first of the type went into public service, nearly fifty NS buses had been built. NS2 was at first an experimental chassis carrying a lorry body and ran under trade plates and it did not become a bus until March 1923 when it was given registration number XR 1442 by which time more than eleven hundred NSs were in service. Some mystery surrounds NS3 and NS4 as they were not supplied to LGOC by AEC until August 1923 when they were registered with the NS500s as XO 9273 and XO 9268 respectively.

347 was new to "East Surrey" on 1 May 1925. It passed to London General Country Services on 7 April 2 and to LGOC on 1 March 1933 (together with routes 411 Sidcup Station to Bromley North Station and Eltham (Well Hall Station) to Orpington) when it arrived at Sidcup (SP) garage with NS1756, 1764, 2348 2349. (J F Higham)

The first of the type to enter service was twenty-two on 10 May 1923 and they were allocated to Hammersmith (R) garage for route 11, Shepherds Bush and Liverpool Street. The actual vehicles were NS 5-8, 10, 12, 15, 17-20, 22-28, 32, 33, 53 and 58. Another twenty six were sent to Hammersmith garage during the remainder of the month.

I clearly remember my first sight of an NS bus and it may well have been early in May 1923 soon after they entered service. My father having a business call in town took my brother and I with him and the first call was in Westminster where to my great surprise I saw these strange new buses on route 11 not having previously read about them in the press. My father then had to go to Fleet Street and he readily agreed that we travel by one of the new NS type buses. The comfortable seats on the lower deck were most noticeable as they had upholstered backs instead of the wooden backs in the earlier K and S type vehicles. I have been told however that some NSs had wooden backs but I have no details as to how many there may have been. Another change was the fitting of windows in the upper part of the front bulkhead and on that first journey I noticed that the driver's head could not be seen from the inside of the bus; this was due to the fact that the bus body was much lower in relation to the cab and engine than in earlier types and necessitated the fitting of a rather attractive white canopy over the driver. The use of the large route stencil, introduced with the S type some two years before, was continued – but only on the front and back of the bus. As the side ventilating windows on the NS were narrow the illuminated stencil boxes for route numbers on each side were quite small. Another change was that due to the reduced space between the top of the driver's cab and the top of the bus the standard type of route board showing six lines of roads or places traversed and in use on all double deck buses since 1909 could not be used on the NS. Instead a wider, three line board showing the same number of names was designed. As these names had to be shown in the direction of travel a hinged board was used that had to be changed by the conductor at each terminal. There was no room for advertisements to be shown on the front of the bus.

NS1 was first built for 52 seats but when fully loaded the maximum permanent axle weight exceeded 3 cwt, so two seats had to be sacrificed, it was however possible to increase to 52 seats later after the fitting of covered top decks. Between May 1923 and October 1924 the introduction of open top NS buses were almost a daily occurrence, a total of 1350 having been produced had entered service. At first they were allocated to the main central London services replacing the S type which were moved to other duties. After route 11, Mortlake (M) garage had them for routes 9 and 73, Tottenham (AR) for 29 and 73, Palmers Green (AD) for 29 and then Battersea (B) and Chalk Farm (CF) which in those days also had an allocation on route 29. This was followed by Seven Kings (AP) for routes 25 and 25A.

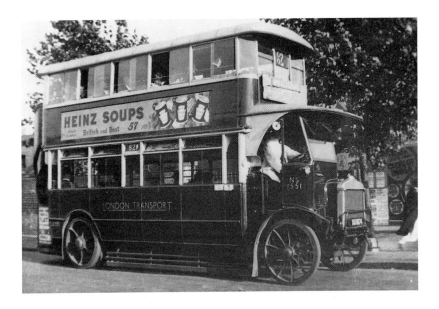

NS1551 was one of the last buses to retain solid tyres for working through Rotherhithe Tunnel. It arrived at Dalston (D) garage on 15 July 1935 and was transferred to Camberwell (Q) garage on 4 March 1936 together with the allocation on route 82.

Gradually the new type spread over much of the General system and allowed many of the B type to be withdrawn. By this time the NS were directly replacing these older B type and I recall this happening on such routes as 1, 4, 49 and 68. The new vehicles were much in evidence during 1924 in dealing with the extra traffic generated by the British Empire Exhibition held at Wembley when the following services were operated entirely by NS, 1, 8, 36A, 49, 68 and 83, mentioning some that are still in existence but other NS routes to Wembley were 58, Wembley and Tottenham, 92 that only ran the short distance to Sudbury Town Station and 93 that then operated south to Putney.

At the time that the first NS was produced it was stated that it would not be available to other operators for some time and, in fact, all NS chassis produced during 1923 and 1924 were taken by the LGOC. The first exceptions were fifteen buses supplied to National Omnibus and Transport Company Ltd., which operated a number of country routes north of London on behalf of the LGOC. They were standard open top NS which were the property of the LGOC even though they carried the fleet name of NATIONAL they had normal fleet numbers. The first were twelve between NS 1024 and NS 1162, new in January – March 1924 and three more NS 1494/5, 1500 four months later. All were registered in Hertfordshire in the NK series and operated mainly from Watford, Hatfield and Hemel Hempstead on routes N2, N3 and N10, the first two later became 301 and 302.

By September 1924 NS1605 had been reached and this was the last chassis delivered direct by AEC with the exception of the fifty six of the 422 type in 1928. All the remainder commencing with NS1606 were built up by LGOC at Chiswick Works or some of the Central Area garages. At this time an order was placed for a further one hundred and thirty two NS numbered 1606 – 1737, the last 13 being intended for National and East Surrey. The latter operated buses south of the Thames on behalf of General. The first East Surrey bus was NS1610 registered as PD 3470, well in advance of the others no doubt for trial purposes. National had six more between NS1606 and 1616. Earlier numbers between 1651 and 1711 were substituted for those ordered as 1725 – 1737 and ten went to East Surrey and three to National. Short Bros built all the bodies for this batch.

By June 1925, buses up to NS1737 had been built for the LGOC but NS1733 was the last to be put into service at the time; the other four chassis were retained for another experiment with covered tops, for in January 1925 General decided to have another attempt to get covered top buses into service in London so Short Bros built four bodies that had more permanent top covers than the NS1 experiment. Upholstered seats were provided on the top deck similar to those inside, together with sliding windows to ensure plenty of ventilation.

NS342 was converted to open top for private hire work. It is seen here at
Stratford working from Putney Bridge (F) garage (where it arrived on
1 May 1933) on route 96 Putney Common – Wanstead (George). Although
withdrawn on 1 July 1933 it was not scrapped until February 1935. (J F Higham)

NS1226 although not a tunnel bus is seen standing at Crystal Palace on route 108
working to Greenwich, Blackwall Tunnel entrance (South) only. This vehicle was
allocated to Old Kent Road (P) garage from July 1930 and is presumably working
on a Whit Monday or August Monday Supplementary Schedule. (E G Masterman)

The first body was completed by 7 July, and after inspection it was decided to go ahead and complete the other three bodies and these were finished late in August in time for operation to commence on route 21 from August 26th. However, following a trial run over the route by NS1734 the police permission to operate covered top buses on the route was withdrawn. Although route 88 was next suggested it was not proceeded with and eventually agreement was reached for the four buses (NS1734-1737, KW 9881-4) to enter service on route 100 on 1st October 1925. The route chosen ran from Loughton to Elephant & Castle.

NS1445 transferred from Hackney (H) garage to Chalk Farm (CF) garage on 12 June 1933, where it stayed until withdrawn in November 1935. It is seen here standing at the Crystal Palace terminal of route 3, awaiting departure to Camden Town. (E G Masterman)

It combined country, suburban as well as town or city roads and was a useful guide to operation. The buses came from Loughton garage and were allocated to duties L3, 8, 11 and 12 the others being standard double deck S type. The experiment was successful as in January 1926 LGOC had permission to build another 200 covered top buses. This was made public as the following extract from a newspaper of early March 1926 clearly shows:

"London is to have 200 covered-top buses. The first four, placed on the Elephant to Epping route, have been so successful that others are being added. Nine more covered buses, our representative was informed yesterday, have now been put on to the streets by the LGOC. They were running on the route from Shepherds Bush to Liverpool Street this weekend. Passengers find them much more comfortable than the old type of bus which is being replaced. There is room for 28 passengers in the padded top deck seats, handrails up the gangways, sliding plate-glass windows, rubber padded – a real luxury vehicle. They do not appear unwieldy and the public are enjoying the experiment of riding in a covered bus, and during a rainy spell, instead of there being a scramble for the inside seats, the competition is to get on top and look at the unfortunate people on the old buses shrinking under waterproof sheets."

NS1590 received its tunnel body with an open staircase on February 1928. It previously saw service at Camberwell (Q), Streatham (AK), Loughton (L) and Merton (AL) garages. It spent the rest of its working life at Athol Street, Poplar (C) garage until withdrawn in April 1937. It is seen here is service on route 108 in LPTB era. (J F Higham)

At the time that the General ordered these 200 covered top buses, an order was also placed for fourteen new open-top NSs for East Surrey and National with bodies by Brush. The covered top vehicles were intended to be NS1739 – 1938 and the 14 open-toppers NS1939-1952. However, the open-top bodies were ready first and so they were mounted on the following chassis – NS1739-43/7/50/2/3/6-8/61/4: the first three went to National and the others to East Surrey, and nearly all were in service before any of the LGOC batch. Consequently, when the first few of the covered-top bodies were completed they were mounted on older chassis that had come in for overhaul, and I recall seeing NS2, 84, 1144, 1184, 1236, 1308, 1312, 1313 and 1647 working on route 11E at the beginning of March 1926 followed during the next few days by NS1219, 1257, 1311, 1659 and 1679. These were soon joined by some new covered top buses such as NS1744, 1745, 1751 etc. It is rather strange that some weeks later when NS1939-1952 came on to the road they had old overhauled open-top bodies and were allocated to various LGOC central area routes at first from Forest Gate and Putney Bridge garages. They all eventually received covered top decks.

The original two hundred covered top bodies, fifty built by Shorts the others by LGOC, could always be distinguished from subsequent deliveries, as they apparently had a heavier roof with internal struts; later bodies had a sheet metal roof without struts. After route 11 these new buses went to Tottenham garage (AR) for routes 29, 76 and 176 and then an allocation to Seven Kings (AP) for the 25 group then Dalston (D) for 9, 11 and 8. Then to several other Central area garages.

So far there has been no mention of NS1738. This vehicle was something of a puzzle; it was not a double deck bus, in fact, it was not a bus at all and the chassis outwardly had little in common with the NS chassis, having a greater resemblance with the ADC 419 type being introduced for private hire coaches; possibly it was given a number in the NS series as it had an NS engine. NS1738, with registration YN 3799, had a coach body and was used for private hire work. Another 'oddity' was NS1953, which had a standard covered top body mounted on a second-hand chassis with the provincial registration of BT 7649 as it was obtained from Hull & District Motor Services.

NS144 was transferred from Hackney (H) garage to Putney Bridge (F) on 19 October 1927 staying there until 30 July 1931. It is seen here on route 39 Southfields Station to Edmonton.

A decision to make the NS chassis available to other operators was made late in 1924 and no doubt this was influenced by the fact that the LGOC was undertaking the construction of so many of their own new vehicles at Chiswick Works thus enabling AEC to utilise their works at Southall for building vehicles for outside sale. From the study of trade papers of the time, it seems that one of the first NS to be sold to another concern was a single bus shipped to Argentina for use in Buenos Aires. This was reported in February 1925, and photographs show a covered-top NS being sent overseas some eight months before covered-top buses were seen in London.

Early in 1925 it was decided that type letters 405, 406, 407 and 408 should be applied to the NS chassis already supplied to the LGOC according to the type of gear box in use. Their chassis numbers were in the continuous series allotted to vehicles supplied to the LGOC and ranged from 22150 to 23759. This was continued for the chassis that were constructed at Chiswick Works. For outside sales by the AEC the chassis numbers commenced at 409001 although NS1953 carries the number 408002. The series reached 409127 by late 1927. In May 1925,

East Surrey purchased eight NSs for use on its own services and, as these were not connected with the General they were not numbered in the LGOC's NS series but carried only the East Surrey fleet numbers 160-167; they had 50 seat open top bodies by Short Bros. and were registered PE 2420-7. Several municipal undertakings bought the 409 type of chassis, including Hull, Liverpool, West Bridgford and Warrington. Hull had two buses with bodies by Short Bros., they were numbered 14 and 15 and registered KH 3428/9; West Bridgford also had two buses but with bodies by Brush. It has not been possible to trace full details of the sales to provincial operators but it seems that most of them had covered top bodies almost identical to those used in London.

NS426 is seen in service on route 148 Leytonstone to Dagenham. It arrived at Leyton (T) garage from Chalk Farm (CF) on 28 April 1927 and stayed there until 14 November 1930 when it moved on to Putney Bridge (F).

Another concern that considered the covered-top 409 type a useful vehicle was Waterloo & Crosby Motor Services Ltd., of Liverpool, which bought eight 52 seat NSs towards the end of 1925 for use on the Seaforth – Crosby route. The bodies were identical with the four then running in London and the Crosby concern was proud of the fact that it possessed eight covered top buses when London only had four. Two more NSs were added later and all ten vehicles eventually passed to Ribble who had obtained a controlling interest in Waterloo & Crosby in 1928. Glasgow General Omnibus & Motor Services of Hamilton, which later became Central SMT Co. Ltd., placed an order for five covered-top 409s with AEC in 1926; these became G1-5 in the fleet which carried the fleet name "G.O.G.", and were registered VA 5706-8, 5743/4. Greyhound of Bristol purchased four or five 409s in 1926 and these eventually passed to Bristol Tramways. Another two were operated by D. Bassett and Sons of South Wales.

It is interesting to note that several of the 409 type were going overseas and in February 1926 two were sold to the Equitable Arts Company of Pittsburg, Pennsylvania, USA; one was an open topper and the other had a covered top, but both had an offside entrance. A story in the trade press shows that in 1926 a London type covered top NS bus travelled right across Europe to Budapest. The bus carried the registration number RM 2561. It appears that this was just a demonstration run and certainly it had a difficult journey, meeting obstacles in the form of bad roads, steep gradients – sometimes as much as 1 in 3 – as well as gateways, arches and overhanging trees. It went by way of Hamburg, Berlin, Leipzig and Bayreuth to Regensburg, but had to complete the journey to Budapest on a barge down the River Danube.

The years 1926 and 1927 were full of activity so far as London was concerned; new covered-top buses, numbered between NS1954 and NS2296 were placed in service and most of the older NSs with open tops had roofs fitted. Route after route was converted to covered-top operation and one did not know which route would be dealt with next; most of the main services in London's centre were changed over quickly, and then some of the outer suburban routes, but it must be remembered that there were still large numbers of the older K and S types which continued as open-toppers and for some time there were a number of routes that the Metropolitan Police would not permit the operation of covered top vehicles. Before a changeover, each route had to be surveyed and it often meant that over-hanging trees had to be cut back.

NS533 arrived at Old Kent Road (P) garage from Upton Park (U) garage on 21 November 1931. It is standing at the Chipstead Valley Road terminus of route 58 ready for the long trip northwards to Camden Town. It was subsequently transferred to Middle Row (X) garage on 1 March 1933.

Some routes had other problems and therefore an interesting experimental vehicle was NS2050, which was designed to work through the Blackwall Tunnel on route 108 – a service operated only by single-deckers. The new double decker covered top of course – had a slightly narrower body than other NSs, which meant that the normal transverse seating arrangement could not be used. Instead, all the seating was longitudinal; that on the lower deck being arranged each side of a central gangway facing inwards, while upstairs it was arranged in 'knifeboard' fashion with a sunken gangway on each side. This enabled the overall height to be lowered by the roof of the lower saloon (or the floor of the upper deck) being carried on specially deeply cranked hoop sticks of light metal section loaded with ash. This allowed headroom in the lower deck under the knifeboard seat of the top deck. The seating was 24 persons in the lower saloon and 22 upstairs but in later examples of the production batch herring-bone bucket seats facing forward at a slight angle were fitted on the upper deck and the total accommodation was reduced to 44. This bus was the first with an enclosed staircase and the roof had a pronounced dome shape to clear the tunnel wall. NS2050 entered service in April 1927 and, six months later, was joined by twenty four similar buses numbered between NS2210 and NS2239. They were put into service on route 108 which was shortened to run only between Bromley-by Bow and Forest Hill as the northern section from Bromley by Bow to Clapton was unsuitable for double deckers due to many low railway bridges. The 108 route later operated to Crystal Palace.

Three other 'odd men out' were NS2051/2/3 which never worked in London. They were three chassis built by LGOC and fitted with standard covered-top bodies and made available to the AEC so that they could fulfil an order for three buses from Greyhound Motors of Bristol. They were registered as HU 8157/8/9 and were later taken over by Bristol Tramways but only one was painted in Bristol colours. One subsequently became a race track totalisator after seeing service in Dublin. Another 'oddment' was NS2231, which the General acquired early in 1927 from a Mr Antichon of Yorkshire; originally a single-decker, with registration number WU 6715, the LGOC fitted it with a covered top body.

The year 1928 saw the introduction of the second of the main improvements to the NS type, when pneumatic tyres made their appearance. The first London double-deckers to be fitted with 'balloon' tyres were the six-wheeled LS of the General and the Guys worked by Public, which appeared in 1927, but such tyres were not permitted on the 4-wheeled NS vehicle until July 1928 after certain regulations had been amended. The difficulty was that the 4-wheeled buses required larger rear tyres which made the NS type wider than the statutory width. Following an increase in the permitted width, the LGOC fitted pneumatics to a number of older NS as well as introducing some new ones. These were some of the later ADC 422 type chassis mounted with a slightly wider body having more luxurious seating and other improvements. The windows on both decks were controlled by individual handles and worked up and down – a great improvement on the horizontal sliding windows of earlier covered-top vehicles. An order for seventy five of these new buses was placed by General but only fifty, numbered NS2297-2346, were delivered. As a matter of fact it was 52 of these new buses that entered service between 2 July and 2 August 1928 as two early ones were included being NS2230 and NS2288, two that had been delayed in completion. These buses were allocated to Cricklewood (W) garage for route 16A, Cricklewood and Victoria and Mortlake (M) for route 33 between Richmond and Aldwych. In May 1929 a further six of the new style bus were introduced and these carried the numbers NS2372-2377, leaving the numbers 2347-2371 unused. These appear to have been diverted to other operators as will be recorded later.

NS642 delivered new to Old Kent Road (P) garage on 4 October 1923, moved to Cricklewood (W) garage on 10 November 1924. It is seen standing in Wembley bus station built by LGOC, to serve the British Empire Exhibition in 1924. Route 36A was a weekday service from Grove Park which commenced on Wednesday 23 April 1924 with an allocation of twenty two NS from Old Kent Road after two shared allocations with Catford (TL) it became entirely Catford from 11 June 1924. Whit Monday 9 June saw an enhanced allocation of Catford (TL) 10 and Cricklewood (W) 21, while August Monday the 4th saw an allocation of Catford (TL) 16 and Camberwell (Q) 38.

Gradually during the next five years a large proportion of the NS fleet were fitted with pneumatic tyres but many were not changed as the NS bus was being replaced by newer types.

A particular advantage of the pneumatic-tyred bus was that its legal speed limit was 20 mph, compared with 12 mph of the solid tyred vehicle, and so pneumatic-tyred buses were to be found on several outer suburban and country routes which could be speeded up. For example routes like 66 that ran along arterial roads such as Eastern Avenue or 121 (later 113) that used the Watford-by-Pass or even the Sunday only 620 on the Kingston-by-Pass could work at the higher speed along such stretches of road. The open-topped NSs operated by National and East Surrey were all converted to pneumatics during 1928.

A rear view of NS2235 one of those with special bodies for working through the Blackwall and Rotherhithe tunnels. It is seen here on route 182 which traversed the Rotherhithe Tunnel on its journey from Stepney to Rotherhithe. (Noel Jackson)

One of the companies operating in London and in association with the LGOC was the British Automobile Traction Co. Ltd., which ran under the fleet name BRITISH and operated 33 buses from a garage in Camden Town on route 24 (Hampstead Heath – Pimlico) and also on Sundays on route 63, (Hampstead Heath – Honor Oak). A fleet of Daimler buses had been used for many years, but during 1927 NS409 type chassis with 48-seat Birch built bodies were introduced as replacements. They were not numbered in the NS series but carried the BAT fleet numbers 501-533 on the bonnets, but when London Transport acquired them in July 1933 they were re-numbered NS2379-2411. They also lost their dark green British livery in favour of the ubiquitous red, but none were ever fitted with pneumatics and all were withdrawn during 1934.

NS1485 joined the "Metropolitan" fleet in February 1928. It was transferred to Clay Hall (Old Ford) (CL) garage when it opened on 7 October 1931. It is seen here taking layover at the Old Ford terminus of route 8, awaiting departure to Colindale Station Underground when working from Clay Hall (CL). (Noel Jackson)

Some NS type buses could be seen in London carrying the fleet name METROPOLITAN; these were vehicles in a separate fleet that was operated by the LGOC on certain selected routes from General garages on behalf of the Tramways (MET)-Omnibus Co.Ltd. In 1927 the MET fleet consisted of K and S type buses but in December that year, twenty one NSs replaced a similar number of S type on route 88A (Acton Green – Mitcham) which was being diverted to work to Grove Park, Chiswick as route 288, which meant running under a low bridge for which the lower NS type was more suitable. The altered routeing did not last long, but the NS vehicles stayed in the Metropolitan fleet and several later received top covers. Early the next year seventy more NSs were transferred from the General to the MET; these were all covered-top vehicles which were then working on routes 8 and 150 between Old Ford and London Bridge or Willesden operating from Willesden and Dalston – later Clay Hall – garages.

Not all the original open topped NSs were given top covers and in 1931 seventy open-toppers remained in use for a few routes with certain restrictions such as 116 and 120. Later five of these buses were transferred to East Surrey, with the operation of route 70 (Morden Station – Dorking) and the remainder were drafted to Old Kent Road garage which at that time could not accommodate full-height buses in part of the garage. Strange to relate the number of open-topped NSs increased during 1932 and 1933 when fifty covered top buses were decapitated some were used on normal services but most were licensed only for private hire work – mainly for operating to the Derby at Epsom where they became ready made grandstands. Another twenty open-toppers were provided in the General fleet in 1932 when some of the former East Surrey and National buses exchanged bodies with covered-top LGOC vehicles; this move resulted in covered top NSs working on country routes for the first time. They mainly ran on routes 303 in the north of London and the 405 in the south. The difficulty with the low roof in Old Kent Road garage was overcome in 1933 so all the open top buses were withdrawn from regular service.

NS2311 was delivered new to Cricklewood (W) garage on 3 July 1928 complete with pneumatic tyres but no glass windscreen. It spent all its working life at Cricklewood until withdrawn in July 1935. It is seen here working on route 121A Mill Hill and Peckham Rye. (Noel Jackson)

NS2387 of the "British" fleet is seen at the Hampstead Heath terminal of route 24. The legal owner is LPTB so this photograph must have been taken between 1 July and 26 July 1933 when the vehicle was withdrawn from service.

The third main development with the NS – a glazed cab to protect the driver – started in 1929. The first experiment in this direction occurred in March with NS198, but does not appear to have been very successful. A modified form of apron windscreen was tried on three more NSs in August and September that year but, after a short time, these were removed leaving the three vehicles with wider than usual driver's cabs. It was some two years before a more satisfactory style of glazed driver's shield was devised and fitted to the NS type buses. Gradually from May 1931 these windscreens became standard on most NS type buses.

Other interesting developments included the fitting of a sliding roof to the top deck of NS397 in 1930 – I have no idea how long this unusual innovation lasted. Also experiments with six-cylinder engines took place, an East Surrey bus, NS1758 based at Reigate was one of them and the other NS2015 a top covered bus on route 60 (Cricklewood – Old Ford) were both fitted with larger engines.

The last NS type bus to enter service in Central London was NS2290, which appeared in February 1930. The chassis had been used at Chiswick for training purposes in the driving school until replaced by an ST chassis – a class then being introduced. The NS was given a covered top body and the late registration number, GC 3953, which was in the middle of a batch of ST registration numbers. It was allocated to Nunhead (AH) garage and I saw it when new running on route 63. It is unfortunate that no illustrations have been traced of this bus or any of the other unusual vehicles, such as NS397, 1953 or 2015.

During its years in operation the NS bus changed considerably in appearance. When introduced in 1923 the open top bus had a large route number stencil box in the centre of the driver's cab canopy and this was illuminated at night. The numbers were quite large and of the style as introduced to London on the S type some three years earlier. Shortly after the renumbering of routes arising from the London Traffic Act, 1924, probably early in 1925 a slimmer style of number appeared permitting a space where a suffix letter could be inserted. 'A', B, 'C' etc. At first the position of the front route number remained the same on the covered-top buses but during 1926 these route numbers were removed to a position above the route boards and in between the two front top deck windows. The conductor could then change numbers when he opened the small door to reverse the route and destination boards. A variation to this occurred in July 1928 with the new style of top deck which had two drop windows in front of top deck. Therefore the route number returned to the centre of the driver's cab canopy. In this connection it should be mentioned that as well as the fifty new buses with the new type of top cover, many older vehicles that were fitted with covered tops after 1928 also had the improved type of top deck with drop window; there were some 250 spread throughout the NS fleet.

NS1549 was fitted with an experimental glass windscreen in September 1929. It is seen here on route 35 Camberwell Green to Highams Park Station at Clapham Common in May 1930. It was transferred from Elmers End (ED) garage on 9 April 1930 to Camberwell (Q) garage where it remained until withdrawn in June 1937. (Noel Jackson)

The wide front route boards which showed up to twelve names of roads or districts served had to be reversed at each terminal so that they read in the direction of travel. This was achieved by a swinging board changed by the conductor. The need for this movement had ceased by about 1930 and the swinging board was removed. Later still the number of names on the board was reduced permitting the extreme destination board to be fitted in at the top.

During the years there had been a change in the position of the GENERAL fleet name. Originally it was shown in the first two panels on each side with suitable border edging in black. After a time the borders were discontinued and later still, the fleet name was repositioned in the centre of the side of the bus.

NS1858 arrived at Forest Gate (G) garage from Cricklewood (W) on 27 March 1929 moving on to Seven Kings (AP) on 4 December 1930. Here it is seen working on route 186 Stratford Broadway to Upminster (Bell).

The use of the illuminated stencil number boxes on the sides were discontinued after the route renumbering of December 1924 when the route numbers were displayed on boards on the upper deck sides in a similar fashion to the older K type bus. With the covered top type these number boards were moved forward below the front upper deck windows. A few years later the use of the illuminated numbers on the centre of the lower deck was resumed.

Mention has been made of the improved NS chassis, designated 422 by the AEC, which were built between 1927 and 1929. In addition to the fifty six buses with this type of chassis that were operated by the General, over a hundred were sold to other operators. The first seventy 422 chassis which had aluminium wheel centres, made up a large order for Anglo-Argentine Tramways. One other chassis went overseas – to Walford Transport of Calcutta – but the others remained in Britain. Newcastle-upon-Tyne obtained six in 1927/8, which became 85-90 in the Corporation fleet and were registered TN 6919 – 6924. Two NSs went to Warrington Corporation being ED 5060/1 and ten to City of Oxford Tramways; which were allocated fleet numbers 104-110 and 1, 7 and 9, their registrations being WL 5337, 5338, 5346, 5347, 5352, 5362, 5363, 5698, 5987 and 6165. The Glasgow General Omnibus Co. Ltd., placed a repeat order for NSs in 1927, and this time had five of the 422 variety which became G6 – 10 (VA 6941-6945). The twenty three buses for these four operators all had 54-seat covered-top bodies built by the LGOC at Chiswick. The last purchaser of the NS type was Derby Corporation, which had six in 1929; these had 48-seat Brush built bodies with enclosed staircase and were numbered 17-22 (CH 7885, 7886, 8337-8340). The only 422 type chassis to carry an open-top body was a demonstrator, which was registered MP 1460; it was, in 1929, added to the East Surrey fleet but was not numbered in the NS series until London Transport days when it became NS2378.

In the first half of 1933, six former East Surrey vehicles passed to the LGOC when it took over the operation of the route between Sidcup and Orpington – then numbered 411 but later part of 51. Three of these buses already had NS numbers, but the others were three of the eight vehicles owned by East Surrey which, it will be recalled, had not carried NS numbers; the General, therefore, issued to them numbers NS2347 – 2349 which had not previously been used.

"British" 518 (NS2396 in LPTB days) is seen here at the Hampstead Heath terminal of route 24 awaiting departure to Pimlico. Note the "British" Daimler to the rear the type of vehicle that the NS type replaced between June and November 1927. It is also interesting to note that Birch Brothers maintained and provided the bodies for the British Automobile fleet tractors.

NS1116 delivered new to Merton (AL) garage on 4 March 1924 as an open topper, is seen here working in later days on route 63A Chalk Farm and Honor Oak from Nunhead (AH) garage (where it resided from 13 December 1930 to 27 February 1931) with a covered top body. (Noel Jackson)

The withdrawal of the NS type in London started in 1932 and nearly 200 had been taken out of service by the time London Transport became responsible for operations on July 1, 1933. Naturally, it was the solid tyred vehicles that were disposed of first, and by January 1935 only 114 buses without pneumatics were in service. Most of these were allocated to Chelverton Road, Putney (AF) garage which could only house covered top buses with solid tyres. After the rebuilding of the garage the number of solid tyred NS were reduced to thirty eight by the end of July 1935. These continued in use until 1937 being required for the special conditions prevailing in the narrow Blackwall and Rotherhithe Tunnels. Blackwall Tunnel, served by route 108, required the specially-designed vehicles that have already been described, there were twenty four of these plus the six of the later delivery. The eight buses in use on route 82 through the Rotherhithe Tunnel were standard covered-top NS except for the solid tyres, which were retained as it was considered there would be excessive wear on pneumatics through the continuous rubbing of the tyre sides on the nearside kerb of the narrow tunnels. One of the special tunnel buses – NS2213 – was fitted with pneumatic tyres in April 1935 to see how they would stand up to the extra wear, none of the others were similarly treated but the experiment was successful and it led to operation of STL type on the tunnel routes and the withdrawal of the solid tyred NS in 1937.

NS1156 was one of the last of its type in service. It is seen here working from Holloway (J) garage (where it arrived on 31 July 1937) on route 4 Finsbury Park Station to Bermondsey (Queen Charlotte). It was withdrawn from service on 5 October 1937.

The year 1937 saw the demise of the NS type in London, at least in passenger service, for during that year they were withdrawn quite rapidly in favour of the new STLs and, by October only 70 were still in use on four routes – 4, (Bermondsey – Finsbury Park), 166, (London Bridge – Aldwych), 178 (Croydon – Addiscombe) and 197, (Croydon – Norwood Junction). It was to route 166 that the doubtful honour fell of bringing to a close another chapter in London's bus history; the end came on the night of November 30, 1937, and, even though it was a wet wintry evening, the final trip from London Bridge Station to Aldwych by NS1974 working from the now closed West Green garage, was suitably celebrated and recorded for posterity.

NS429 was withdrawn in March 1937 and converted for use as a mobile canteen, and became 32H in the miscellaneous service vehicle fleet. It was allocated to Hackney (H) garage in October 1937 and it is possibly seen here at the Stoke Newington terminal of route 73. It moved on to Nunhead (AH) in January 1938 and to Hammersmith (R) in June. In August 1939 it returned to Hackney (H) and was delicensed in October. It was relicensed into Holloway (J) in July 1940 moving to Finsbury Park Station in the August, being delicensed again in June 1941. It was relicensed into Putney Bridge (F) in June 1942 for a few days before moving on to Camberwell Tram Depot. The next move was to Victoria (GM) in July 1946 where it stayed a year going to Merton (AL) its final base in July 1947, being withdrawn in April 1948.

However, as has often been the case, a number of NS buses found a 'new life' in other spheres; thirteen were sold to a Mr Middlemiss of Upminster, who used them to take poor East End children on outings to the London countryside. London Transport retained some 25 NS for use on other duties. The Tramways Department had nine, which were fitted with special bodies and used as tower wagons. Four had their bodies adapted for use as tree-cutting vehicles. The other twelve saw another 10-14 year's service as staff canteens, with the lower deck fitted out as the kitchen/servery and the upper deck as a 'restaurant'. These mobile canteens were at first painted green, but later red. In 1940 all 25 were allotted numbers 20H – 44H in the service vehicle fleet.

I have no record of any other NS type vehicle having remained in use after withdrawal from service in London and the well known survivor of the class is NS1995 (YR 3844) one of the relics in the London Transport Collection. It is a standard covered-top double-decker with pneumatic tyres introduced in February 1927 and, therefore, had ten years active service in London, but has now been in honourable retirement for over fifty years. It remains to remind us of a most interesting type of motorbus, which – in the twenties at least – certainly was in many respects "Nulli Secondus".

LS TYPE MOTOR BUS

The first indication that as I expect did most Londoners at the time have of the proposed introduction of six-wheeled buses into London was the press release in the morning papers one day in May 1927. I retained the cutting from that paper and it reads:- "London bus to hold sixty-eight. Six-wheeled vehicle built by the LGOC."

"A six-wheeled General omnibus fitted with covered top and pneumatic tyres and holding sixty-eight passengers will shortly be seen on the London streets if Scotland Yard agrees."

"Drawings of the vehicle were submitted to the licensing authorities several months ago. It has now been built, and subject to its passing the police tests will be put into operation as an experiment".

"To be known as the "London Six", the new bus will be equipped with a 35 horse power Daimler sleeve-valve engine. The horse/power of the original "B" type bus was 28 and its seating capacity thirty-four".

The first photographs of LS1, showed the bus with boards for route 11E, Shepherds Bush and Liverpool Street. Yet when it eventually entered service a few weeks later on 4th June 1927 it was not on route 11E but 16A It was allocated to Cricklewood (W) garage and ran as 'W 23' on the short but busy route between Cricklewood "The Crown" and Victoria Station. It was not only the first six-wheeled bus in London but also the first double deck to have pneumatic tyres, although they had been in use on single deckers on some suburban routes for nearly two years. At that time there were about 1400 covered top buses operated by the LGOC, all being of the NS type, but none of them had by then been fitted with pneumatic tyres. This was due to a restriction in the permitted width of buses which was not relaxed until July 1928. On the four-wheeled NS type the heavy tyres on the rear wheels projected out too much whereas the six-wheeler had two standard size wheels at the rear. So that LS1 was in operation with some sixty solid tyred NS type buses which then worked route 16A. LS1 had the registration number YH 1200 and the words LONDON SIX shown under the LS fleet number.

LS1 had a Chiswick built body very similar to the standard covered top NS type of that time. The top deck windows were of the "slide along" type and the front route number was carried in slots above the extreme destination board. The seating on both decks was of the standard NS pattern, wood framed with upholstered seats and backs. The ADC bonnet and drivers shield differed considerably from that on the NS type of bus. The enclosed staircase, another novelty on the LS was not entirely new to London as a specially built NS bus with similar shaped enclosed staircase had been produced and in service just a few weeks earlier on the Blackwall Tunnel route 108.

This view of LS2 shows the enclosed staircase 66 seat version. It was delivered new to Cricklewood (W) garage on 29 July 1927 for service on route 16A Cricklewood (Crown) to Victoria Station. It was transferred to Palmers Green (AD) on 12 February 1928 for service on the 29 group of routes and was exchanged for LS9 with Tottenham (AR) on 8 December 1928 for service on the 69 group. In February 1929 it became an open staircase 64 seater and moved on to Mortlake (M) garage for service on route 33. It returned to Tottenham (AR) on 9 April 1930 for service on the 29 group moving to Cricklewood (W) on 24 September that year for service on 16A. It became a 60 seater in April 1931, and a 56 seater in July 1934. It was withdrawn in October 1936. (London Transport U45631)

Guy Motors had also been experimenting with a six-wheeled double deck bus for use in London and one of these was on order but did not enter service until 9 September 1927. This was the first new double decker for the London Public Omnibus Company and as GS1 it was put on to route 529 between Winchmore Hill and Victoria.

LS2 entered service on 20 August 1927, just a short time before the Guy six-wheeler and this second large ADC bus was also put on route 16A so as to join LS1. Six drivers and six conductors from Cricklewood garage had been trained as crews for these new buses. The fact that LS2 had a lower registration number, YH 1166, whereas LS1 was YH 1200 needs some explanation. The reason is that the LGOC at times used the blocks of registration numbers allotted to them from "both ends", so while YH 1101 onwards was used for the standard NS type then entering service, numbers from YH 1200 in reverse order were used for experimental and service vehicles.

Although the press report had said that LS1 had 68 seats in fact LS1 had at first 66 seats and LS2 had 64 seats.

The chassis for the LS type was ADC model 802 and twenty chassis were built in 1927 and 1928 and were given chassis numbers 802001 to 802020. LS1 and LS2 were 802001 and 802003. The second 802 chassis was adapted for another purpose not being used as a service bus at all. The LGOC built for it a body to hold 104 passengers being 59 on the upper deck and 45 downstairs. This was at the time AEC were in the process of moving from Walthamstow in North East London to Southall some twenty miles away on the western outskirts and it was necessary to provide transport for works and office staff. At first a fleet of B type buses had been used but this large LS bus replaced many of the smaller vehicles. Not being used for public service it was not subject to control by the Metropolitan Police. The upper deck was extended further over the driver's canopy and rear facing back seats for five persons were fitted at the front on both decks. Another seat was squeezed in under the stairs and about seventeen extra passengers were accommodated on tip-up seats in the gangways. Additional emergency exit was provided by a door at the front nearside of the upper deck with a steel ladder to the ground. It operated on trade plates and began operation in July 1927.

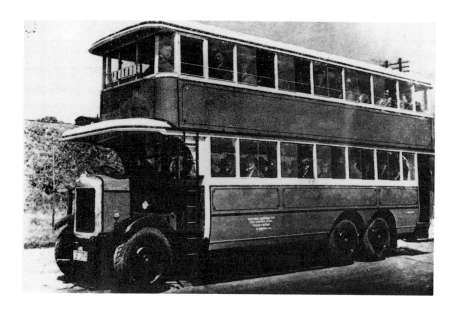

This 104 seater LS was used by AEC to take staff to and from Walthamstow to the new factory at Southall which was officially opened in October 1927. It supplemented a fleet of twenty four B type buses fitted with cape cant hoods and seating for 40 passengers. The first window and section of the upper deck on the nearside was an emergency exit in the form of a door – the rope ladder for descent can just be seen in this illustration.

The next three chassis 802004-6 were demonstrators supplied to provincial operators with bodies by Short Bros. They went to Westcliff on Sea Motor Services (HJ 7670) in October 1927, Maidstone & District Motor Services (KO 5702) in August 1927, and also in August to Southdown Motor Services (UF 2638). Another AEC works bus came next this was 802007 which was practically the same as the earlier large bus except it was a 102 seater. It was built by the LGOC in September 1927.

Short Bros built the bodies for two more demonstrators 802008 and 802010. The first went to Birmingham Corporation in December 1927 being OX 4594. The other was supplied to Sheffield Corporation in May 1928 and was registered as WE 2205. Chassis 802009 although built in April 1928 never received a body and was dismantled by the LGOC for spares in August 1929.

The remaining chassis 802011-20 constructed during 1928, were retained by the LGOC and put into service during the year. LS3 was sent to Cricklewood (W) garage on 9 February 1928 for route 16A and no doubt the three buses provided useful data on the working of large and pneumatic tyred buses in conjunction with the solid tyred NS bus. It was certainly interesting in those days as one never knew which type would come along.

LS4 and 5 were registered together and they went into service in May 1928 on two other routes. LS4 was sent to Palmers Green (AD) garage and worked on route 29A Southgate "The Crown" and Victoria Station. LS5 went to Mortlake (M) garage for route 33A Waterloo Station and Richmond. These were two vastly different routes to the more or less straight run of the 16A and so much more experience was gained in their operation. As with the 16's these other routes were at that time worked with solid tyred NS vehicles.

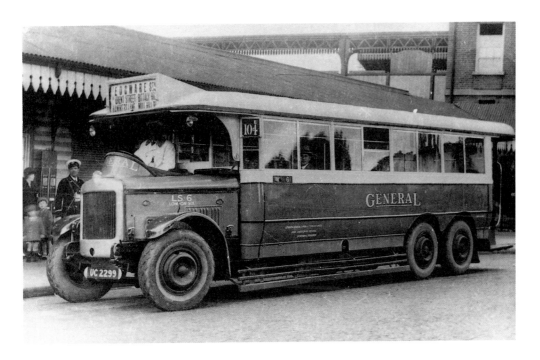

LS6 was a 34 seat single decker delivered new to Cricklewood (W) garage on 19 July 1928. It first saw service on route 16A and transferred to route 104E Golders Green Station Underground to Edgware Station on 6 February 1929. This became route 240 on 3 October 1934 and LS6 worked on this service until withdrawn in April 1935. It was then converted to breakdown lorry 219U and allocated to Hammersmith (R) on 6 May 1936 and stayed there until withdrawn in July 1950. (J F Higham)

LS6 was a single decker having a 34 seat rear entrance body and it spent all its working life allocated to Cricklewood (W) garage and at first ran on route 16A to Victoria Station with the other LS buses and it was not until February 1929 that it was put on to a single deck route. This was 104E Mill Hill and Golders Green (later numbered 240), which was then worked with single deck K type buses with solid tyres due to the low bridge at Mill Hill Station. LS7 entered service shortly before the single deck LS6 and was sent to Mortlake (M) on 30 June to join LS5 on the 33A route. The bodies of LS1-5/7 were of the same pattern although varying in seating from 64 to 70 at first. But the bodies of the last five LS were of an improved type and they were built about the same time and to a similar design to the last fifty bodies for the NS type which were mounted on NS2297 – 2346. These were the first NS to have pneumatic tyres and they went into service from July 1928 from Cricklewood (W) and Mortlake (M) and thus joined the LS type on routes 16A and 33A. The seating on these bodies were much more comfortable and more like the seating that we have become used to on later types of bus. The windows, both upstairs and down were controlled by handles and worked "up and down" and during hot weather I considered they were the best ventilated of any covered top bus. Similar windows being fitted at the front on the top deck meant that the front route number had to be returned to the centre of the driver's canopy, where it had been on all buses previously except for most of the NS covered top type. Three of these buses, LS9, 10 and 11 entered service in September 1928 being sent to Tottenham (AR) garage and worked on route 69B Edmonton and Camberwell Green and this was extended to Herne Hill in peak hours as 369B. LS8 built in July 1928 was first used as a demonstrator and a photograph shows it in the livery of Greenock and Fort Glasgow Tramways when it had an enclosed staircase. It was eventually sent to Mortlake (M) on 2 October 1928 thus joining LS5 and LS7 on the 33A route. Finally LS12 also joined them on 3 January 1929 so that four six-wheelers were to be seen working through Kensington and Barnes. LS8 to 12 all had 70 seats. By February 1929 Palmers Green (AD) had two LS buses for route 29 as LS7 one of the double deckers at Mortlake had been transferred. In June 1929 the Tottenham allocation on 69/369 routes was passed to the London Public Omnibus Company and so LS9, 10 and 11 moved to Mortlake garage increasing the LS type on the 33 route to seven.

I have not been able to confirm exactly how many of the double deck LS bodies were built with the enclosed staircase, maybe all except LS12 but as the enclosed staircase in Central London was not looked on favourably by the Metropolitan Police it seems that by the end of 1928 all had been converted and rebuilt with open staircase as on the standard NS bus.

LS8 is seen working on route 33 to Richmond during its stay at Mortlake (M) garage from new on 2 October 1928 as a closed staircase 72 seater. It was converted to an open staircase 70 seater in January 1929 and is seen here in that form. It also went to Tottenham (AR) on 9 April 1930 for service on the 29 group of routes and to Cricklewood (W) on 24 September that year to work on 16A. It was converted to a 60 seater in May 1931 and to a 56 seater in March 1935. It was withdrawn in March 1937, and rebodied as a Breakdown Lorry by the Eagle Engineering Co. of Warwick. It entered service as 220U in the miscellaneous service vehicle fleet at Dalston (D) in January 1936. It was finally withdrawn in July 1950. (F Higham)

On the 9th April 1930 the duties on the 29 group of routes were revised and a section extended to Potters Bar. All eleven double deck LS type buses were then based at Tottenham (AR) garage so they worked exclusively on the 29A between Southgate and Victoria. The route was again reallocated upon the introduction of the winter schedules on 8 October 1930 and the Potters Bar extension was handed over to Overground who ran it as 629. All eleven LS buses were once more re-allocated and moved to Cricklewood (W) garage and for the remainder of their working life operated between Cricklewood 'Crown' and Victoria Station on 16A, the route on which operation had started in 1927. In 1934 the seating on these double deck LS was reduced to sixty passengers. LS6 the single decker was withdrawn from service in June 1935 as by that time the single deck LT type was in use. The double deck LS type were gradually withdrawn between October 1936 and early 1937 the final four disappearing from the 16s in February 1937.

Further use was made of LS6 as in May 1936 it was rebuilt as a 9-ton heavy breakdown tender for towing broken down buses etc. Two years later three more became breakdown tenders, they were LS8 in January 1938, LS3 in February and LS10 in March. In 1940 they were numbered 219U, 220U, 221U and 222U respectively in the London Transport service fleet. All four were sold to Lammas Motors, dealers in April 1951. They had served longer as breakdown tenders than they had as buses.

Another vehicle with an interesting history was 802006 (UF 2638) which had been returned from Southdown in 1928 and on 2 May 1929 it was sent to East Surrey Traction Company at Reigate as a 60-seat open top bus, and numbered 45 in the East Surrey fleet. It was returned to the LGOC in July 1930 given a lorry body and numbered as LS13. On the 23 March 1932 it was sold to the London Electric Railway for use at the Underground railway works at Acton, having their fleet number 22. It stayed there until it was scrapped in 1935. The Sheffield demonstrator 802010 was destroyed by fire in about 1929. The two AEC works buses and the other three demonstrators having been returned to the AEC passed to the Walthamstow Wayfarers Club at dates not known.

From February 1929 LS6 was transferred to work on route 104E Golders Green to Edgware, and is seen here leaving Golders Green bound for Edgware

APPENDIX A
CHASSIS NUMBERS

A new series of chassis numbers was started by AEC with the K type which commenced at 20001. The numbers 20504 – 20753 were at first reserved for sales to other operators but as only twenty-eight chassis were actually sold most of the remaining numbers were used for later deliveries to the LGOC. Eventually the numbers 20680 – 20753 were cancelled. Numbers 21004 to 21019 and 21270 to 24567 were given to S and NS chassis supplied to the LGOC. Outside sales not included.

20001 – 20003	K1 – 3	August 1919, September 1919	(K3 used as an instructional chassis at Chiswick, never fitted with a body.)
20004 -20503	K4 – K503	May 1920 – December 1920	
20504	Demonstrator		registration number not known
20505 – 20510	Torquay Tramways	January 1921	registrations numbers: TA 1004 – 1006, 1168 -1170. To LGOC November 1926 as K1127 – K1132
20511 – 20550	K1004 – K1043	April 1921	
20551 – 20554	K1063 – K1066	April 1924	
20555 – 20560	East Surrey	July 1920	registrations numbers XB 8264/7, 8386, 8403/31/42 and fleet numbers 27-32
20561 – 20571	K1067 – 1077	April 1924	
20572 – 20573	K1078 – K1079	July 1925	
20574	Demonstrator		registration number not known
20575	Robinson of Scarborough		registration number AJ 7584 on 7th January 1922
20576	Demonstrator, single deck		registration number: XB 9084. Also known to have been demonstrated to Robinson of Scarborough 5th June 1922
20577	Demonstrator		registration number not known
20578	Demonstrator		registration number LF 9243

In November and December 1921 twenty-five chassis were supplied to the LGOC by AEC for dismantling and used for replacement of certain K types, an R follows in the listings against these numbers.

20579, 20580	K548 R, K874 R	
20581	K1044	July 1921
20582, 20583	K645 R, K504 R	
20584	K1045	July 1921
20585, 20586	K768 R, K628 R	
20587	K489 R	
20588 – 20589	Unknown operator, but sold by AEC 31st December 1920. (20589 registered NO 2114, 7th May 1921.)	
20590	K718 R	
20591	K663 R	
20592 – 20594	K1060 – K1062	July 1921
20595	K663 R	
20596, 20597	K886 R, K742 R	
20598, 20599	K563 R, K714 R	
20600	K613 R	
20601	Robinson of Scarborough	registration number: AJ 7587 on 7th January 1922
20602, 20603	K524 R, K762 R	
20604	K626 R	
20605		Demonstrator. registration number XH 3021
20606	K662 R	
20607 – 20610	K1047 – K1050	July 1921
20611	K557 R	
20612	K1046	August 1921
20613, 20614	K526 R, K486 R	
20615, 20616	K477 R, K863 R	
20617 – 20624	K1051 – K1058	July 1921
20625	K1059	August 1921
20626 – 20633	K1080 – K1087	July 1925 – August 1925
20634	K566 R	
20635 – 20648	K1088 – K1101	August 1925 – December 1925
20649 – 20651	K1102 – K1104	August 1926

20652 – 20657	East Surrey	March 1921	registration numbers: PB 9558 – 9563 and fleet numbers 24-25, 33/34, 23
20658 – 20679	K1105 – K1126	August 1926 – September 1926	
20680 – 20753	Cancelled		
20754 – 21003	K504 – K753	December 1920 – February 1921	
21004	T1	April 1920	
21005	S1	September 1920	
21006 – 21019	S2 – S15	February 1921	
21020 – 21269	K754 – K1003	February 1921 – April 1921	
21270	S16	July 1921	
21271 – 22149	S17 – S895	July 1921	
22150	NS1	August 1922	
22151 – 23004	NS2 – NS855	March 1923	
23005	S896	June 1923	
23006 – 23505	NS856 – NS1355	September 1923	
23506 – 23508	S897 – S899	August 1923	
23509	S900		Nothing known of this vehicle
23510 – 23759	NS1356 – NS1605	May 1924	
23760	S901	September 1924	
23761	S902	February 1925	
23762 – 23775			Other Operators ??
23776 – 23907	NS1606 – NS1737	September 1924	
23908			Other Operator ??
23909 – 24123	NS1738 – NS1952	March 1926	
24124 – 24149			Other Operators ??
24150 – 24424	NS1954 – NS2228	November 1926	
24425 – 24449	S903 – S927	February 1927	
24450 – 24497	NS2232 – NS2279	October 1927	
24498 – 24499	NS2229 – NS2230	December 1927	
24500 – 24501	NS2280 – NS2281	May 1928	
24502	S928	November 1927	
24503 – 24567	NS2282 – NS2346	May 1928	

BODY NUMBERS, DATES TAKEN INTO STOCK AND BUILDERS OF K, S, NS & LS

4587	January 1918	K1		LGOC
4588	June 1919	K2		LGOC
4639 – 4788	September 1919 – August 1920	K	D/D	LGOC North Road
4789 – 4888	August 1920 – December 1920	K	D/D	Short
4889 – 5088	April 1920 – February 1921	K	D/D	Brush
5089 – 5098	June 1920	K	D/D	LGOC Seagrave Road
5099 – 5108	July 1920	K	D/D	Brush
5109 – 5113	August 1920	K	D/D	LGOC Seagrave Road
5114 – 5138	September 1920 – November 1920	K	D/D	Brush
5217	April 1920	T1	D/D	LGOC, body later to S10
5218	July 1920	K	D/D	LGOC North Road
5220 – 5256	August 1920 – September 1920	K	D/D	LGOC North Road & Seagrave Road jointly
5257	September 1920	S1	D/D	LGOC
5258 – 5399	September 1920 – November 1920	K	D/D	LGOC North Road & Seagrave Road jointly
5400 – 5599	December 1920 – April 1921	K	D/D	Short
5600 – 5699	December 1920 – May 1921	K	D/D	Strachan
5700 – 5705	November 1920	K	D/D	LGOC North Road
5706 – 5758	December 1920 – March 1921	S	D/D	LGOC North Road
5759 – 5902	April 1921 – October 1921	S	D/D	LGOC North Road, Seagrave Road & Chiswick jointly
5909 – 5923	October 1921	S	D/D	LGOC as 5759 – 5902
5925	December 1921	K	D/D	LGOC Experimental
5926	December 1921	S	S/D	LGOC Experimental 34 seats
5927 – 5935	July 1922 – August 1922	S	S/D	LGOC Chiswick
5936 – 5938	August 1922	S	S/D	Short
6013 – 6112	March 1921 – June 1921	K	D/D	Dodson
6113 – 6161	June 1921 – September 1921	S	D/D	Dodson
6162 – 6211	December 1920 – February 1921	K	D/D	Brush

6212	September 1921	S	D/D	Dodson. Follows 6161 to complete order for 50 buses
6263	April 1921	S	D/D	Brush
6264 – 6313	May 1922 – July 1922	S	D/D	Dodson
6314 – 6513	May 1922 – September 1922	S	D/D	Short
6514	March 1922	S265	S/D	LGOC Chiswick. (All LGOC bodies built at Chiswick from here on.)
6515 – 6531	September 1922 – October 1922	S	S/D	Short
6532 – 6596	September 1922 – November 1922	S	D/D	Short
6597	May 1922	S	D/D	LGOC
6598 - 6647	July 1922 – October 1922	S	D/D	Dodson
6648 – 6650	June 1922	S	S/D	LGOC
6651	August 1922	S	D/D	LGOC
6652	August 1922	NS1		LGOC Built as covered top but not used in service and converted to open top.
6653 – 6697	November 1922 – March 1923	S	D/D	LGOC
6698 – 6701	March 1923	S	S/D	LGOC
6702 – 6776	January 1923 – February 1923	S	D/D	Short
6777 – 6801	February 1923 – March 1923	S	D/D	Ransomes
6804				Charabanc body fitted to S896 (this body sold April 1928 and replaced on S896 with standard D/D body.)
6805 – 6830	March 1923 – July 1923	S	S/D	LGOC
6831 – 6905	March 1923 – April 1923	S	D/D	Short
6906 – 7055	March 1923 – August 1923	NS		LGOC
7056 – 7315	April 1923 – July 1923	NS		Short
7316 – 7500	May 1923 – September 1923	NS		Brush
7501 – 7700	July 1923 – October 1923	NS		Short
7701 – 7765	August 1923 – September 1923	NS		LGOC
7766 – 7789	June 1923	PS		Ransomes (National PS5-13)
7790 – 7792	July 1923	S	D/D	Ransomes
7793 – 7942	September 1923 – February 1924	NS		LGOC
7943 – 8042	November 1923 – April 1924	NS		Ransomes
8043 – 8292	November 1923 – May 1924	NS		Short
8293 – 8295	October 1923	S	D/D	Ransomes
8296 – 8470	May 1924 – September 1924	NS		Short

8471 – 8545	June 1924 – November 1924	NS		Brush
8546	March 1924	S	S/D	LGOC
8547 – 8571	April 1924 – July 1924	NS		LGOC
8578 – 8607	April 1924 – June 1924	PS		Ransomes (ESTC PD 1348-72, 9752-56)
8611 – 8620	September 1924	NS		Short
8650 – 8791	November 1924 – August 1925	NS		Short
8792 – 8891	April 1925 – October 1925	K	D/D	Short
8893 – 8898	July 1925	K	S/D	LGOC
8900 – 8904	July 1925	K	D/D	LGOC
8911	September 1925	K	S/D	LGOC
8912	July 1925	NS1738		LGOC Special single deck body.
8913 – 8948	September 1925 – December 1925	K	S/D	LGOC
8950 – 8999	March 1926 – June 1926	NS		Short
9000 – 9013	January 1926 – March 1926	NS		Short
9014 – 9038	January 1926 – February 1926	NS		LGOC
9039	December 1925	K	S/D	LGOC
9040 – 9164	February 1926 – June 1926	NS		LGOC
9165 – 9172	February 1926	PS		LGOC (ESTC PE 8309-14, National PS14, 15.)
9272 – 9323	April 1925 – June 1926	K	S/D	LGOC
9330 – 9354	June 1926	K	S/D	LGOC
9360	June 1926	NS1953		Ex Hull & Dist. M.S. BT 7649 in exchange for Dennis XX 670
9362 – 9461	August 1926 – February 1927	NS		LGOC
9509 – 9667	February 1927 – July 1927	NS		LGOC (Includes 9534, Tunnel type NS2050.)
9674 – 9683	August 1927	NS		LGOC
9684 – 9696	April 1927	S	S/D	LGOC (S915-927)
9697 – 9708	January 1927	S	D/D	LGOC (S903-914)
9709 – 9732	September 1927 – October 1927	NS		LGOC Tunnel type
9733 – 9756	November 1927	NS		LGOC Tunnel type
9760 – 9767	March 1927	PS		LGOC (ESTC PF 9016 – 23)
9780 – 9781	December 1927	NS		LGOC
9787 – 9804	April 1927 – May 1927	K	S/D	LGOC
9852 – 9853	December 1927	NS		LGOC
9857	December 1927	NS		LGOC
9863	May 1927	LS1		LGOC 66 seater reduced later to 60 seats.)

9864	July 1927	LS		LGOC (104 seat ADC staff bus.)
9865	October 1927	LS		LGOC (104 seat ADC staff bus.)
9932	July 1927	LS2		64 seater reduced later to 60 seats.
9938	December 1927	LS4		LGOC 70 seater reduced to 60 seats
9939		NS2378		LGOC. Body sold by AEC to Greenock & Port Glasgow Tramways Co. Re-taken into LGOC stock 15th May 1929 and sent to ESTC. NS number allotted 1933.
9975	December 1927	LS3		LGOC 70 seater later reduced to 60 seats.
9976	December 1927	LS5		LGOC 70 seater later reduced to 60 seats.
10005 – 10019	April 1928	NS		LGOC
10065 – 10068	May 1928	NS		LGOC
10069 – 10070	May 1928	NS		LGOC Prototype 7'5" wide bodies
10071	May 1928	LS7		LGOC 70 seater reduced later to 60 seats.
10072	February 1928	LS6		LGOC 34 seat single deck.
10099 – 10103	June 1928 – July 1928	LS		LGOC LS8-12 all 70 seats later to 60 seats.
10107 – 10156	May 1928 – June 1928	NS		LGOC 7'5" wide
10169 – 10170	April 1929	K	S/D	LGOC 30 seaters
10179 – 10184	April 1929	NS		LGOC 7'5" wide
10201	May 1929	LS13		Taken into stock ex Southdown
10202 – 10207	July 1929	NS		LGOC Tunnel type.

K TYPE TRANSFERRED FROM LGOC TO INDEPENDENTS

List showing the LGOC K type which replaced the various Independent buses in 1926 and 1927. They were allocated to the LGOC garages as shown by the code letters. Although Cambrians carried the code CA they were operating from HW garage. Several others worked out of E the Invicta garage and EH the Atlas garage, East Ham. The routes shown in the last column are those on which the bus was licensed to operate. The K type replacements during 1926 were painted in the livery and with the fleet names of the respective companies, but from January 1927 they all regained the GENERAL red livery and fleet name with the name of the Independent company shown on the lower panel as legal owner.

Date	Name	K type	In replacement for	Garage	Route Worked
20/2/26	Central	K11, 42, 70, 980	Straker Squire	J	27A
22/2/26	Shamrock	K650, 947, 1038	Thornycroft	AF	14
20/3/26	Fleet	K163	(temporary loan – to Cambrian)		
20/3/26	Edward Paul	K329	(temporary loan – to Cambrian)		
14/4/26	Cambrian	K295, 329 (ex EP)	Thornycroft	CA	185 & 291
15/4/26	Cambrian	K163 (ex Fleet)	Thornycroft	CA	185 & 291
16/4/26	Cambrian	K95	Thornycroft	CA	185 & 291
17/4/26	Cambrian	K80, 118, 325, 447	Thornycroft	CA	185 & 291
26/4/26	Ubique	K412	Thornycroft	G	101A
27/4/26	R A	K458	Daimler	H	6A
27/4/26	Olympic	K89	Thornycroft	C	15A
1/6/26	Royal Blue	K127, 143, 204, 284	Straker Squire	X	247
3/6/26	Royal Blue	K155	Straker Squire	X	247
8/6/26	Royal Blue	K381	Dennis	X	247
17/8/26	Horseshoe	K206	Leyland	AR	29
17/8/26	Royal Blue	K311	Leyland	X	247
18/8/26	Fleet	K712, 787	Straker Squire	AH	12C
16/9/26	Cambrian	K837	Straker Squire	CA	185 & 291

17/9/26	Cambrian	K610	Straker Squire	CA	185 & 291
2/10/26	Cambrian	K844	Straker Squire	CA	185 & 291
6/11/26	Legion	K903	Thornycroft	R	112B
26/11/26	Clarence	K754	Dennis D24	B	526
27/11/26	Fleet	K986	Dennis D23	AH	23C
30/11/26	Primrose	K805	Dennis D26	AR	69A
30/11/26	Royal Blue	K691, 924	Straker Squire	X	247
4/12/26	Western	K611	Dennis D25	W	60 & 247
6/12/26	Direct	K756	Dennis D27	AR	525
7/12/26	Clarence	K200	Dennis D28	AH	25B
13/12/26	Criterion	K809	Dennis D29	AR	29
21/12/26	Cambrian	K672	Straker Squire	CA	185 & 291
4/1/27	Super Bus	K769	Dennis D30	F	14A
18/1/27	Empress	K1003	Thornycroft	CF	294
21/1/27	Cambrian Landray	K119, 124, 833, 851, 904	Tilling Stevens	P	159A
24/1/27	Western	K569	Dennis D31	W	60 & 247
24/1/27	Florence	K5	Dennis D34	R	49A
25/1/27	Fleet	K722	Dennis D33	AH	12C
25/1/27	Florence	K320	Dennis D35	R	49A
27/1/27	Western	K450	Dennis D32	W	60 & 247
28/1/27	Imperial	K1041	Dennis D36	AR	59A
2/2/27	Ubique	K572	Leyland	G	101A
2/2/27	Western	K975	Dennis D37	W	60 & 247
2/2/27	Grafton	K945	Dennis D38	T	511B
3/2/27	Tower	K967	Thornycroft	B	88
4/2/27	A1	K993	Dennis D39	AH	12C
9/2/27	Alberta	K308	Leyland	J	206 & 525
1/3/27	Tower	K211	Thornycroft	B	73A
7/3/27	Tower	K185	Thornycroft	B	73A
7/3/27	Primrose	K74	Straker Squire	AR	69A
7/3/27	Edward Paul	K1037	Straker Squire & two Leyland	AH	12C
8/3/27	Edward Paul	K18, 901	Straker Squire & two Leyland	AH	12C
10/3/27	Edward Paul	K20, 65, 459	Straker Squire & two Leyland	AH	12C
11/3/27	Edward Paul	K67, 92, 174, 156, 715	Straker Squire	J	27A

14/3/27	Victoria Road Car	K227	Straker Squire	J	27A
15/3/27	Edward Paul	K598, 1008	Straker Squire & two Leyland	AH	12C
15/3/27	Marathon	K104, 167	Leyland	S	185
17/3/27	Western	K344	Straker Squire	W	60 & 247
18/3/27	Lonsdale	K416	Daimler Y	R	73E
21/3/27	Cambrian	K148	Straker Squire	CA	185 & 291
21/3/27	Lonsdale	K139	Daimler Y	R	73E
31/3/27	Horseshoe	K171	Daimler Y	AR	29
31/3/27	The Lea Rig	K160	Daimler Y	F	14A
1/4/27	White Star/ Monarch	K103	Daimler Y	AR	69A
2/4/27	Celtic	K1069	Daimler Y	R	73E
8/4/27	Western	K188	Straker Squire	W	60 & 247
12/4/27	Cambrian	K290, 307, 324	Straker Squire	CA	185 & 291
21/4/27	Western	K142	Straker Squire	W	60 & 247
21/4/27	Cambrian	K413	Straker Squire	CA	185 & 291
22/4/27	Cambrian	K129	Straker Squire	CA	185 & 291
23/4/27	Cambrian	K109	Straker Squire	CA	185 & 291
25/4/27	Cambrian	K172, 209, 212, 401	Straker Squire	CA	185 & 291
26/4/27	Cambrian	K81, 212, 465, 531	Straker Squire	CA	185 & 291
1/7/27	Empress	K210	Leyland	CF	294
13/7/27	Empress	K195	Dennis D47	CF	294
14/7/27	Atlas	K519, 561	Leyland	EH	15 & 23
15/7/27	Invicta	K196	Leyland	E	23
16/7/27	Invicta	K473	Leyland	E	23
18/7/27	Invicta	K478	Leyland	E	23
19/7/27	Invicta	K713	Leyland	E	23
21/7/27	Vivid	K335	Leyland	EH	25
22/7/27	Alberta	K334	Leyland	J	206 & 525
30/7/27	Uneedus	K927, 1098 both single deck	Guy single deck	AR	551
13/9/27	Orange	K567, 1129	Dennis single deck	CF	550
14/9/27	Orange	K1130	Dennis single deck	CF	550
15/9/27	Orange	K692, 730, 914, 923	Dennis single deck	CF	550
30/9/27	Jockey	K485	Leyland	T	511B
6/10/27	Britannia	K622	Leyland	EH	15E
6/10/27	Atlas	K707, 729	Leyland	EH	15 & 23

7/10/27	Tottenham Hotspur	K642	Leyland	AR	69A
8/10/27	Wellington	K499	Leyland	T	511A
11/10/27	Tottenham Hotspur	K654	Leyland	AR	69A
12/10/27	Wellington	K471	Leyland	T	511A
12/10/27	Orange	K675	Leyland	W	27A
13/10/27	Britannia	K488	Leyland	EH	15E
13/10/27	Tottenham Hotspur	K629	Leyland	AR	15E
13/10/27	Atlas	K724, 908	Leyland	EH	15 & 23
14/10/27	Atlas	K436, 522	Leyland	EH	15 & 23
15/10/27	Atlas	K802	Leyland	EH	15 & 23
17/10/27	Atlas	K435, 537, 688, 1124	Leyland	EH	15 & 23
19/10/27	Britannia	K502	Leyland	EH	15E
20/10/27	Britannia	K727, 897	Leyland	EH	15E
20/10/27	Atlas	K786, 910	Leyland	EH	15 & 23
21/10/27	Tottenham Hotspur	K566	Leyland	AR	69A
21/10/27	Atlas	K832	Leyland	EH	15 & 23
22/10/27	Orange	K665	Leyland	W	27A
24/10/27	Grangewood	K686	Leyland	E	23
24/10/27	Orange	K666	Leyland	W	27A
24/10/27	Tottenham Hotspur	K928	Leyland	AR	69A
25/10/27	Loveland	K593	Leyland	AR	73E
25/10/27	Atlas	K663	Leyland	EH	15 & 23
26/10/27	Cosgrove	K568	Leyland	AR	69A
15/12/27	P C	K60	Dennis D41	T	511B
16/2/28	Cambrian	K85	Straker Squire	CA	185 & 291
16/4/28	Cambrian	K149	Straker Squire	CA	185 & 291
18/4/28	Cambrian	K84, 88	Straker Squire	CA	185 & 291
19/4/28	Cambrian	K108	Straker Squire	CA	185 & 291

The Thornycrofts were all sold to Thames Valley. The five Tilling Stevens were passed to Thomas Tilling for use with the Timpson fleet that they had taken over. The Dennis after overhaul and numbering in the D class were included in the fleet of Redburns another Independent taken over by LGOC. The Orange Dennis single decks were replaced by double deck K type due to the change in operation of route 550.

APPENDIX D
NS TYPE BODY NUMBERS

At first over 1750 NS bodies were built as open top due to the fact that London Police would not accept a covered top deck. This changed after four covered top buses, NS1734 to NS1737 were tried out in London in 1925. Commencing in 1926 some 500 new covered top bodies were built either mounted on new chassis or on to older chassis which had been fitted with open top bodies. Eventually nearly all the open top bodies had been rebuilt as covered top with a few exceptions as shown in the following summary

Chassis		Bodies	
NS1	1	Body number 6652 built as covered top but not used in service and converted to open top	1
NS2-NS5	4	Bodies fitted later	
NS6-NS855	850	6906-7765 includes 10 spare bodies	860
NS856-NS1355	500	7793-8292 (included 14 National)	500
NS1356-NS1605	250	8296-8545, 8547-8571 includes 25 spare bodies (included 3 National)	275
NS1606-NS1733	128	8611-8620, 8650-8791 includes 20 spare bodies	
		(included 9 National and 11 East Surrey)	148
NS1739- 43/47/50/52/53/ 56-58/61/64	14	9000-9013 (3 National and 11 East Surrey)	14

ADDITIONAL OPEN TOP BUSES

NS1939-NS1952	14	Fitted with spare open top bodies	
NS1953	1	9360	1
NS2179-NS2182, NS2204	5	9675-9679	5
NS2284/85	2	10067/68 (National)	2
NS2378	1	9939 (East Surrey)	1
	1770		1807
		Bodies which remained open top, viz 65 Central area, 31 National and 27 East Surrey	123
		Total bodies rebuilt as covered top between 1926 and 1929	1684

COVERED TOP BUSES

NS1734-NS1737	4	8788-8791	4
NS1744/45/46/48/39/51/	186	8950-8999 (15 on new chassis and 35 on old chassis)	

54/55/59/60/62/63/65-NS1938			
(149 with new bodies and 37 old bodies)		9014-9038 (25 on new chassis)	
		9040-9164 (71 on new chassis and 54 on old chassis)	200
NS1954-2178/83-2203/5-28 (238 with new bodies and 32 old bodies)		9362-9461, 9509-9667, 9674/80-83	264
(NS2050, 2210/12-14/16-18/20-28/32-39)	270	9709-9756 (44 seat clerestory tunnel type)	48
NS2229-NS2231	3	9780/9781, 9852/53/57	5
NS2232-83/86-NS2346	111	10005-10019, 10065-10068	19
		10069/70, 10107-10156 (7'5" wide)	52
NS2372-NS2377	6	10179-10184 (7'5" wide)	6
		10202-10207 (tunnel type)	5
	580		599
Single-deck 30 seater saloon for private hire			
NS1738	1	8912	1

Difficult to identify, this is probably number 142 of July 1924 origin, an AEC PS. Possibly it is standing at its Uckfield terminus ready to depart on the long haul to West Croydon; the route south of Forest Row was lost by the 1933 London Transport Act.

KEY TO THE FOLLOWING ABBREVIATIONS

S20S	20 seat single deck with solid tyres.
S22P	22 seat single deck with pneumatic tyres, Morden type.
S24P	24 seat single deck with pneumatic tyres.
S24P/E	24 seat single deck with pneumatic tyres, with East Surrey at first.
S24P/N	24 seat single deck with pneumatic tyres, with National at first.
S24S	24 seat single deck with solid tyres.
S30P	30 seat single deck with pneumatic tyres
S30	30 seat single deck with solid tyres later fitted with pneumatics.
ESTC	East Surrey Traction Company Ltd vehicles
MET	Tramways (MET) Omnibus Company Ltd (Metropolitan)
NAT	National Omnibus Company Ltd. vehicles
SMET	South Metropolitan Electric Tramways

NOTE:

Initial garage allocations are shown in these lists. Unfortunately at the present time the Chiswick 'cards' for most of the K class have not been located.

LS6 was the only single deck representative of its class. It was delivered to Cricklewood (W) garage on 19 July 1928, and entered service on route 16A (Cricklewood (Crown) to Victoria). It is seen here outside Cricklewood garage awaiting its turn for refuelling, cleaning, etc. (A B Cross/W Noel Jackson)

K	Reg No.	Garage	Remark	K	Reg No.	Garage	Remark	K	Reg No.	Garage	Remark
1	LU 8231	R		62	LU 8269			123	LU 8387		
2	LU 8232	AP		63	LU 8282			124	LU 8340		
3	UC 2221			64	LU 8277			125	LU 8330		
4	LU 8242		S20S	65	LU 8357			126	LU 8339		S22P
5	LU 8245			66	LU 8304			127	LU 8327		
6	LU 8239			67	LU 8379			128	LU 8346		
7	LU 8234			68	LU 8297			129	LU 8338		
8	LU 8256			69	LU 8281			130	LU 8443		
9	LU 8243			70	LU 8287			131	LU 8335		
10	LU 8233			71	LU 8280			132	LU 8332		
11	XF 8014			72	LU 8299			133	LU 8326		
12	LU 8238			73	LU 8380		S22P	134	LU 8444		
13	LU 8249			74	LU 8301			135	LU 8331		S22P
14	LU 8235			75	LU 8290			136	LU 8445		
15	LU 8271			76	LU 8381			137	LU 8446		
16	LU 8237			77	LU 8296			138	LU 8447		
17	LU 8240			78	LU 8300			139	XC 9710		Originally Lorry
18	LU 8276			79	LU 8382			140	LU 8498		S30P
19	LU 8236			80	LU 8305			141	LU 8402		
20	LU 8248			81	LU 8303			142	LU 8400		
21	LU 8246			82	LU 8378			143	LU 8342		
22	LU 8247			83	LU 8377			144	LU 8343		
23	LU 8241			84	LU 8376			145	LU 8333		
24	LU 8257			85	LU 8394			146	LU 8399		
25	LU 8274			86	LU 8298			147	LU 8334		
26	XF 8084			87	LU 8294			148	LU 8329		
27	LU 8250			88	LU 8295			149	LU 8344		
28	LU 8244			89	LU 8293			150	LU 8321		
29	LU 8284			90	LU 8395			151	LU 8391		S22P
30	LU 8270			91	LU 8396			152	LU 8345		
31	LU 8261			92	LU 8397			153	LU 8438		
32	LU 8356		S22P	93	LU 8398			154	LU 8392		
33	LU 8258			94	LU 8279			155	LU 8350		
34	XF 8079			95	LU 8314			156	LU 8322		
35	LU 8272			96	LU 8421			157	LU 8323		
36	LU 8263			97	LU 8422			158	LU 8324		
37	LU 8253			98	LU 8423			159	LU 8349		
38	LU 8286			99	LU 8315			160	LU 8325		
39	LU 8267			100	LU 8311			161	LU 8413		
40	LU 8268			101	LU 8307			162	LU 8427		
41	LU 8266		S20S	102	LU 8309			163	LU 8414		
42	LU 8251			103	LU 8312			164	LU 8475		
43	LU 8275			104	LU 8310			165	LU 8348		
44	LU 8260			105	LU 8313			166	LU 8352		
45	LU 8252		S24P	106	LU 8319			167	LU 8389		
46	LU 8254			107	LU 8320			168	LU 8401		
47	LU 8255		S20S	108	LU 8317			169	LU 8477		MET
48	LU 8264			109	LU 8347			170	LU 8404		
49	LU 8278			110	LU 8318			171	LU 8415		
50	LU 8288			111	LU 8424			172	LU 8403		
51	LU 8259			112	LU 8302			173	LU 8419		S30P
52	LU 8273		ESTC	113	LU 8316			174	LU 8416		
53	LU 8285			114	LU 8441			175	LU 8430		
54	LU 8269		S20S	115	LU 8442			176	LU 8468		MET
55	LU 8283		ESTC	116	LU 8358			177	LU 8409		
56	LU 8499			117	LU 8336			178	LU 8412		
57	LU 9292 8292			118	LU 8337			179	LU 8390		
58	LU 8308			119	LU 8367			180	LU 8405		
59	LU 8291			120	LU 8328			181	XP 4181		
60	LU 8265			121	LU 8341			182	LU 8429		
61	LU 8262			122	LU 8306			183	LU 8448		

K	Reg No.	Garage	Remark	K	Reg No.	Garage	Remark	K	Reg No.	Garage	Remark
184	LU 8418			245	LU 8455			306	LU 8549		
185	LU 8406			246	XC 8055			307	LU 8517		
186	LU 8408			247	XC 8061			308	XF 8082		
187	LU 8410			248	XC 8024			309	LU 8580		
188	LU 8425			249	XC 8033			310	LU 8534		MET
189	LU 8407			250	XC 8077			311	XC 8021		
190	LU 8426			251	XC 8027			312	LU 8581		
191	LU 8420			252	XC 8084		MET	313	XC 8073		
192	LU 8483			253	XC 8085			314	LU 8494		MET
193	LU 8417			254	LU 8547		MET	315	LU 8556		
194	LU 8411			255	LU 8458			316	LU 8542		
195	LU 8470			256	LU 8551		MET	317	LU 8582		
196	LU 8469			257	LU 8481			318	LU 8530		
197	LU 8439			258	LU 8393			319	LU 8476		S20S
198	LU 8431			259	LU 8459			320	LU 8583		
199	LU 8428			260	LU 8375			321	LU 8535		MET
200	XF 8080			261	LU 8577			322	XC 8009		
201	LU 8471			262	LU 8460			323	LU 8560		
202	LU 8433			263	LU 8461			324	LU 8584		
203	LU 8437			264	LU 8372			325	LU 8599		
204	LU 8436			265	LU 8462			326	LU 8514		
205	LU 8435			266	LU 8546		MET	327	LU 8585		
206	LU 8473			267	LU 8527		MET	328	LU 8495		
207	LU 8480			268	LU 8500		MET	329	LU 8586		MET
208	LU 8351			269	LU 8386			330	LU 8485		MET
209	LU 8432			270	LU 8528			331	LU 8564		
210	LU 8457			271	LU 8463		S22P	332	LU 8543		MET
211	LU 8353			272	LU 8545		MET	333	LU 8496		
212	LU 8370			273	LU 8385			334	LU 8478		
213	LU 8369			274	LU 8529			335	LU 8484		
214	LU 8474			275	LU 8368			336	LU 8513		
215	LU 8467		S20S	276	LU 8501			337	LU 8562		
216	LU 8384			277	LU 8464		ESTC	338	LU 8488		
217	LU 8434			278	LU 8363			339	LU 8512		
218	LU 8364			279	LU 8502			340	LU 8558		S20S
219	LU 8374			280	LU 8578			341	LU 8544		S20S
220	LU 8451			281	LU 8505			342	LU 8561		MET
221	LU 8449			282	LU 8554			343	LU 8587		ESTC
222	LU 8373			283	LU 8506			344	XF 8081		
223	LU 8365			284	LU 8465			345	LU 8486		MET
224	LU 8454			285	LU 8523		S22P	346	XF 8083		
225	LU 8466			286	LU 8479			347	LU 8489		
226	LU 8383			287	LU 8524			348	XC 8036		
227	LU 8355			288	LU 8552		S24S	349	LU 8538		
228	LU 8526			289	LU 8548			350	LU 8588		
229	LU 8354			290	LU 8503			351	LU 8510		
230	LU 8359			291	LU 8515			352	LU 8507		
231	LU 8388			292	LU 8553			353	LU 8557		
232	LU 8361			293	LU 8504			354	LU 8566		
233	LU 8440			294	LU 8491		MET	355	LU 8519		
234	LU 8452			295	LU 8492			356	LU 8511		
235	LU 8366			296	LU 8555		MET	357	LU 8490		
236	LU 8362			297	LU 8525		MET	358	LU 8508		
237	LU 8550			298	LU 8487		MET	359	LU 8509		
238	LU 8450		MET	299	LU 8493			360	LU 8571		S22P
239	LU 8456		S22P	300	LU 8579			361	LU 8516		
240	LU 8453			301	XC 8007			362	XC 8047		S30P
241	LU 8360			302	LU 8559		MET	363	LU 8539		
242	LU 8472			303	LU 8482			364	LU 8563		MET
243	LU 8371			304	XC 8008			365	LU 8597		
244	LU 8497			305	LU 8522		MET	366	LU 8598		

103

K	Reg No.	Garage	Remark	K	Reg No.	Garage	Remark	K	Reg No.	Garage	Remark
367	LU 8594			427	XC 8038			488	XC 8104		
368	LU 8540			428	XC 8078			489	XC 8119		S30P
369	XC 8010		MET	429	XC 8050		ESTC	490	XC 8127		
370	LU 8532		MET	430	XC 8046			491	XC 8096		MET
371	XC 8004			431	XC 8020			492	XC 8100		MET
372	LU 8600			432	XC 8039		MET	493	XC 8111		MET
373	XC 8011			433	XC 8040		MET	494	XC 8113		S20S
374	XC 8012		S22P	434	XC 8076		SMET	495	XC 8103		MET
375	LU 8592			435	XC 8041			496	XC 8109		S24S
376	XC 8013			436	XC 8064		S30P	497	XC 8134		MET
377	XC 8014			437	XC 8051			498	XC 8123		
378	XC 8031		S24S	438	XC 8042			499	XC 8128		
379	LU 8595			439	XC 8035			500	XC 8116		
380	LU 8589		S22P	440	XC 8030			501	XC 8138		
381	LU 8565			441	XC 8045			502	XC 8117		
382	LU 8518			442	XC 8043			503	XC 8122		
383	LU 8569			443	XC 8048			504	XC 8112		
384	LU 8520			444	XC 8034			505	XC 8108		
385	XC 8002 (8022?)			445	XC 8029			506	XC 8130		
386	LU 8531			446	XC 8081		MET	507	XC 8121		
387	LU 8591			447	XC 8065			508	XC 8124		
388	LU 8593		S22P	448	XC 8044			509	XC 8126		S22P
389	XC 8015			449	XC 8023		MET	510	XC 8120		
390	XC 8001			450	XC 8052			511	XC 8142		
391	XC 8002 (8022?)			451	XC 8053			512	XC 8136		
392	LU 8537		MET	452	XC 8066			513	XC 8145		S22P
393	LU 8533		MET	453	XC 8049			514	XC 8131		MET
394	LU 8596			454	XC 8067			515	XC 8135		
395	LU 8521		S22P	455	XC 8088			516	XC 8137		
396	LU 8573		S22P	456	XC 8060			517	XC 8118		
397	XC 8016			457	XC 8080			518	XC 8146		
398	LU 8575			458	XC 8068		MET	519	XC 8143		
399	XC 8003			459	XC 8056			520	XC 8132		
400	LU 8536		S20S	460	XC 8054			521	XC 8133		
401	LU 8570			461	XC 8074			522	XC 8129		
402	LU 8541		MET	462	XC 8089			523	XC 8125		
403	XC 8017			463	XC 8075			524	XC 8144		
404	XC 8005			464	XC 8069		ESTC	525	XC 8147		
405	XC 8018		MET	465	XC 8070			526	XC 8148		
406	LU 8568			466	XC 8071			527	XC 8186		S24S
407	XC 8032		MET	467	XC 8072			528	XC 8163		
408	LU 8572			468	XC 8082			529	XC 8140		
409	LU 8576			469	XC 8097			530	XC 8139		
410	XC 8028		MET	470	XC 8091			531	XC 8141		
411	LU 8590			471	XC 8110			532	XC 8148		
412	XC 8006			472	XC 8083		SMET	533	XC 8149		S22P
413	XD 8311			473	XC 8079			534	XC 8160		S20S
414	XC 8025			474	XC 8101		S24S	535	XC 8159		
415	LU 8574			475	XC 8106		MET	536	XC 8165		
416	LU 8567			476	XC 8098		MET	537	XC 8150		
417	XC 8057		MET	477	XC 8114			538	XC 8151		MET
418	XC 8026			478	XC 8090			539	XC 8161		
419	XC 8019			479	XC 8093		SMET	540	XC 8177		
420	XC 8086		SMET	480	XC 8099			541	XC 8157		MET
421	XC 8062		MET	481	XC 8105		SMET	542	XC 8156		MET
422	XC 8037		MET	482	XC 8102			543	XC 8152		
423	XC 8058			483	XC 8107			544	XC 8158		
424	XC 8059		SMET/ MET	484	XC 8094		MET	545	XC 8162		
				485	XC 8095			546	XC 8153		
425	XC 8063			486	XC 8115		S20S	547	XC 8154		MET
426	XC 8087		SMET	487	XC 8092		S20S	548	XC 8175		MET

K	Reg No.	Garage	Remark	K	Reg No.	Garage	Remark	K	Reg No.	Garage	Remark
549	XC 8182			610	XC 8225		MET	671	XC 8473		
550	XC 8166			611	XC 8234			672	XC 8243		
551	XC 8301			612	XC 8470		MET	673	XC 8288		
552	XC 8187			613	XC 8272			674	XC 8242		MET
553	XC 8181			614	XC 8215		MET	675	XC 8259		S30P
554	XC 8164			615	XC 8427		S20S	676	XC 8491		S24S
555	XC 8167			616	XC 8221		MET	677	XC 8539		MET
556	XC 8155			617	XC 8241			678	XC 8429		
557	XC 8169		MET	618	XC 8433			679	XC 8474		
558	XC 8171			619	XC 8226		MET	680	XC 8268		
559	XC 8173		MET	620	XC 8299			681	XC 8428		
560	XC 8168			621	XC 8235		S20S	682	XC 8247		
561	XC 8194			622	XC 8296			683	XC 8262		
562	XC 8198		SMET	623	XC 8217		MET	684	XC 8305		
563	XC 8232			624	XC 8223			685	XC 8333		
564	XC 8178			625	XC 8227		MET	686	XC 8281		
565	XC 8170			626	XC 8273			687	XC 8260		S20S
566	XC 8202			627	XC 8236		MET	688	XC 8245		S30P
567	XC 8180			628	XC 8220			689	XC 8246		
568	XC 8199		MET	629	XC 8237		MET	690	XC 8244		MET
569	XC 8189			630	XC 8230		MET	691	XC 8306		
570	XC 8174			631	XC 8238			692	XC 8289		
571	XC 8191			632	XC 9711			693	XC 8401		
572	XC 8172			633	XC 8301			694	XC 8263		
573	XC 8203		MET	634	XC 8400			695	XC 8335		
574	XC 8204			635	XC 8302		MET	696	XC 8250		MET
575	XC 8185		MET	636	XC 8303		MET	697	XC 8439		MET
576	XC 8233		MET	637	XC 8231			698	XC 8274		
577	XC 8193			638	XC 8471		MET	699	XF 8015		
578	XC 8196		MET	639	XC 8291		S22P	700	XC 8396		
579	XC 8176			640	XC 8489		MET	701	XC 8430		
580	XC 8205			641	XC 8422			702	XC 8325		MET
581	XC 8206		MET	642	XC 8338		MET	703	XC 8458		MET
582	XC 8192		S22P	643	XC 8249			704	XC 8297		
583	XC 8207			644	XC 8228		MET	705	XC 8265		S20S
584	XC 8190			645	XC 8238			706	XC 8275		MET
585	XC 8188			646	XC 8457			707	XC 8264		
586	XC 8195		SMET	647	XC 8252			708	XC 8420		
587	XC 8208		MET	648	XC 8253		MET	709	XC 8269		
588	XC 8213			649	XC 8254		MET	710	XC 8310		MET
589	XC 8209			650	XF 8012		MET	711	XC 8276		
590	XC 8251			651	XC 8385		MET	712	XC 8270		
591	XC 8211		MET	652	XC 9758			713	XC 8267		
592	XC 8179			653	XC 8435		MET	714	XC 8277		S20S
593	XC 8214			654	XC 8239			715	XC 9713		
594	XC 8200			655	XC 8436			716	XC 8387		MET
595	XC 8336		MET	656	XC 8437			717	XC 8475		MET
596	XC 8210			657	XC 8358			718	XC 8278		MET
597	XC 8212		MET	658	XF 8032	AC		719	XC 8279		
598	XC 9744			659	XC 8248			720	XC 8389		MET
599	XC 8216			660	XC 8304			721	XC 8431		
600	XC 8219		MET	661	XC 9712			722	XC 8463		
601	XC 8261		MET	662	XC 8255		MET	723	XC 8440		
602	XC 8218			663	XC 8240			724	XC 8290		
603	XC 8490		MET	664	XC 8438		MET	725	XC 8363		MET
604	XC 8197		S20S	665	XC 8332		S30P	726	XC 8441		MET
605	XC 8292		S30P	666	XC 8472			727	XC 8282		
606	XC 8271			667	XC 8256			728	XC 8380		MET
607	XC 8222		MET	668	XC 8298		MET	729	XC 9742		
608	XC 8224		S20S	669	XC 8257			730	XC 8283		
609	XC 8229			670	XC 8258		MET	731	XC 8330		

K	Reg No.	Garage	Remark	K	Reg No.	Garage	Remark	K	Reg No.	Garage	Remark
732	XC 8311		MET	793	XC 8339		S20S	854	XC 9784		
733	XC 8284		MET	794	XC 8372			855	XC 8447		
734	XC 8312			795	XC 8356			856	XC 8498		
735	XC 8313			796	XC 8360			857	XC 8448		
736	XC 8280			797	XC 8355			858	XC 8449		MET
737	XC 9714			798	XC 8373			859	XC 9760		S24P/N
738	XC 8316		S20S	799	XC 8351			860	XC 9718		
739	XC 8476			800	XC 8477		MET	861	XC 8450		
740	XC 8314		MET	801	XC 8354			862	XC 8451		
741	XC 8285		MET	802	XC 8465			863	XC 8452		MET
742	XC 8350		S20S	803	XC 8395			864	XC 8453		
743	XC 8286		MET	804	XC 8362			865	XC 8454		
744	XC 8364			805	XC 8405			866	XC 8455		
745	XC 8381			806	XC 8443			867	XC 8432		
746	XC 8295			807	XC 8374			868	XD 8310		
747	XC 8287		S30P	808	XC 9759			869	XC 8456		SMET
748	XC 8317			809	XC 8406			870	XC 8434		
749	XC 9743			810	XC 8423		S24S	871	XC 8478		
750	XC 8293			811	XC 8384		MET	872	XC 9747		
751	XC 8318			812	XC 8407			873	XC 8499		
752	XC 8492			813	XF 8033			874	XC 8459		
753	XC 8319			814	XC 8408			875	XC 8460		
754	XC 8365			815	XC 8377			876	XC 8461		
755	XC 8294			816	XC 8375		MET	877	XC 9756		
756	XC 8320			817	XC 8409		S24P	878	XC 8479		MET
757	XC 8402		MET	818	XC 8378			879	XC 8480		MET
758	XC 9715		S20S	819	XC 8414			880	XC 8500		
759	XC 8321			820	XC 8417			881	XC 8462		
760	XC 8493		MET	821	XC 8379			882	XC 8481	B	
761	XC 8322			822	XC 8388			883	XC 8785	H	
762	XC 8324			823	XC 8383			884	XC 9701	X	
763	XC 8366			824	XC 8386		MET	885	XC 9772	H	MET
764	XC 8367		MET	825	XC 9771			886	XC 8482	B	
765	XC 8421			826	XC 9745			887	XC 8483	B	
766	XC 8323			827	XC 8410			888	XC 8464	B	
767	XC 8403			828	XC 8399			889	XC 9719	X	
768	XC 8353		MET	829	XC 9716		MET	890	XC 8466	B	
769	XC 8300			830	XC 8411			891	XC 8484	B	
770	XC 8416			831	XC 8390		S24P/N	892	XC 8467	B	
771	XC 8404			832	XC 8418			893	XC 8469	B	
772	XC 8368			833	XC 8444			894	XC 9702	X	
773	XC 8315		S24P/N	834	XC 8412			895	XC 9740	X	
774	XC 8369		MET	835	XC 9717			896	XC 8468	B	S24P/N
775	XC 8326		MET	836	XC 8413			897	XC 9757	H	
776	XC 8442		MET	837	XC 8391			898	XC 8485	B	
777	XC 8329			838	XC 8495		S20S	899	XC 9773	H	MET
778	XC 8327			839	XC 8392			900	XC 9720	X	MET
779	XC 8376			840	XC 8394		MET	901	XC 8487	B	
780	XC 8370			841	XC 8496			902	XC 9748	X	
781	XC 8331			842	XC 8397			903	XC 9703	AL	
782	XC 8371			843	XC 8398		S20S	904	XC 9721	X	
783	XC 9741			844	XC 8415			905	XC 8488	B	
784	XC 8337			845	XC 8393			906	XC 9786	H	
785	XC 8494		MET	846	XC 9746			907	XC 9787	H	
786	XC 9783			847	XC 8445		MET	908	XC 9739	X	
787	XC 8334			848	XC 8426		MET	909	XC 9761	H	MET
788	XC 8361			849	XC 8419			910	XC 9722	X	
789	XC 8486			850	XC 8425			911	XC 9749	X	
790	XC 8382			851	XC 8497			912	XC 9704	B	S24P
791	XC 8357			852	XC 8424			913	XC 9723	X	MET
792	XC 8352		S20S	853	XC 8446			914	XF 8016	G	

K	Reg No.	Garage	Remark	K	Reg No.	Garage	Remark	K	Reg No.	Garage	Remark
915	XF 9017 [8017]	AC		976	XC 9799	H	S20S	1037	XF 8072	Q	
916	XC 9788	H	S20S	977	XC 9780	H	MET	1038	XF 8073	Q	
917	XC 9705	B		978	XF 8031	AC		1039	XF 8074	Q	S20S
918	XF 8018	AC		979	XC 9781	H		1040	XF 8075	Q	
919	XC 9706	AL	MET	980	XC 9800	H		1041	XF 8076	Q	
920	XC 9707	AL	S20S	981	XF 8001	H		1042	XF 8077	Q	S24S
921	XC 9750	X		982	XF 8009	H		1043	XF 8078	R	
922	XC 9724	X		983	XF 8035	AC		1044	XD 8308	AP	S22P
923	XC 9762	H		984	XC 9782	H	MET	1045	XD 8305	AP	
924	XC 9725	X		985	XF 8002	H		1046	XD 8312	B	S205
925	XC 9726	X	MET	986	XC 9755	H		1047	XD 8303	AP	
926	XC 9708	X		987	XF 8003	H		1048	XD 8304	AP	
927	XC 9727	X	S24P/N	988	XF 8024	AC		1049	XD 8301	AL	
928	XC 9709	AL	MET	989	XF 8004	H		1050	XD 8302	AL	
929	XC 9728	AL	S24S	990	XF 8005	H		1051	XF 8093	AL	S20S
930	XC 9763	H		991	XF 8036	AC		1052	XF 8096	AL	S20S
931	XC 9729	AL		992	XF 8006	H		1053	XF 8094	AL	S24P/N
932	XC 9751	X		993	XF 8010	H		1054	XF 8097	AL	S24S
933	XC 9730	X		994	XF 8007	H		1055	XF 8098	AL	S24S
934	XC 9731	AL		995	XF 8011	H		1056	XF 8095	AL	S20S
935	XC 9732	X		996	XF 8025	AC	S24P/N	1057	XF 8099	AL	
936	XC 9733	R		997	XF 8026	AC	S20S	1058	XF 8100	AL	
937	XC 9734	X		998	XF 8027	AC		1059	XD 8377	East Surrey	
938	XC 9752	X		999	XF 8028	AC					
939	XC 9735	X	MET	1000	XF 8037	AC		1060	XD 8307	AP	S24S
940	XC 9736	X		1001	XF 8038	AC		1061	XD 8306	AP	
941	XC 9737	X		1002	XF 8029	AC		1062	XD 8309	AP	S24S
942	XF 8019	AC		1003	XF 8030	AC		1063	XR 4289	W	S24S
943	XC 9789	H	S20S	1004	XF 8042		S24P/N	1064	XR 4290	W	S24S
944	XF 8020	AC		1005	XF 8043	R		1065	XR 9926	W	S20S
945	XC 9738	X	MET	1006	XF 8044	Q	S20S	1066	XR 9919	W	S24S
946	XF 8034	AC		1007	XF 8039	AC		1067	XR 9917	W	S24S
947	XF 8201 [8101?]	AC		1008	XF 8040	AC		1068	XR 9920	W	S24S
948	XC 9790	H		1009	XF 8057	Q		1069	XR 9918	W	
949	XC 9754	H		1010	XF 8058	Q	MET	1070	XR 9921	W	
950	XF 8022	AC	S20S	1011	XF 8045	Q	MET	1071	XR 9927	W	
951	XF 8008	H		1012	XF 8046	Q	MET	1072	XR 9941	W	S24S
952	XC 9774	H	S20S	1013	XF 8047	Q		1073	XR 9942	W	S24S
953	XC 9791	H		1014	XF 8048	Q		1074	XR 9943	W	
954	XF 8023	AC		1015	XF 8059	Q	S24S	1075	XR 9953	W	
955	XC 9775	H		1016	XF 8049	Q	S20S	1076	XR 9954	W	
956	XC 9764	H		1017	XF 8050	Q	S20S	1077	XR 9961	W	
957	XC 9765	R		1018	XF 8051	Q		1078	XW 9867	AV	S24P
958	XC 9766	H		1019	XF 8060	Q		1079	XW 9870	AV	S24P
959	XC 9792	H		1020	XF 8041	Q		1080	XW 9871	AV	S24P
960	XC 9793	H		1021	XF 8061	Q		1081	XW 9872	AV	S24P
961	XC 9753	H	S20S	1022	XF 8062	Q		1082	XW 9873	AV	S24P
962	XC 9794	H		1023	XF 8063	Q		1083	XW 9874	AV	S24P
963	XC 9795	H	S24S	1024	XF 8064	Q		1084	XW 9875	K	S24P
964	XC 9767	H		1025	XF 8052	Q		1085	XW 9876	K	S24P
965	XC 9796	H		1026	XF 8053	Q	S24P/N	1086	XW 9877	K	S24P
966	XF 8013	H	S24P/E	1027	XF 8054	Q		1087	XW 9878	K	S24P
967	XC 9768	H		1028	XF 8055	Q	S20S	1088	XW 9879	K	S24P
968	XC 9776			1029	XF 8065	Q		1089	XW 9880	MH	S20S
969	XC 9769	R		1030	XF 8056	Q		1090	XW 9885	K	S24P
970	XC 9777	H		1031	XF 8066	Q		1091	XW 9886	K	S24P
971	XC 9797	H		1032	XF 8067	Q		1092	XW 9887	K	S24P
972	XC 9778	H	MET	1033	XF 8068	Q	S24S	1093	YL 8051	MH	S20S
973	XC 9770	H	MET	1034	XF 8069	Q	S20S	1094	YL 8052	K	S24P
974	XC 9779	H	MET	1035	XF 8070	Q	S20S	1095	YL 8054	K	S24P
975	XC 9798	H		1036	XF 8071	Q	S2OS				

K	Reg. No.	Garage	Remark	K	Reg. No.	Garage	Remark	K	Reg. No.	Garage	Remark
1096	RO 2072		NAT	1113	YP 6634	AC			**EAST SURREY K TYPE**		
			S24P/N	1114	YP 6649	P					
1097	RO 2071		NAT	1115	YP 6650	W		23	PB 9563		
			S24P/N	1116	YP 6659	P		24	PB 9558		
1098	RO 2070		NAT	1117	YP 6660	W		25	PB 9559		
			S24P/N	1118	YP 6661	AC		26	PB 9560		
1099	YL 8053	K	S24P	1119	YP 6675	AM		27	XB 8264		
1100	YL 8055	A	S24P	1120	YP 6676	J	S30P	28	XB 8267		
1101	YL 8056	A	S24P	1121	YP 6684	AC		29	XB 8386		
1102	YP 6606	AC		1122	YP 6693	H		30	XB 8403		
1103	YP 6607	AB		1123	YR 3806	H		31	XB 8431		
1104	YP 6608	AB		1124	YR 3807	AH		32	XB 8442		
1105	YP 6609	B		1125	YR 3808	R		33	PB 9561		
1106	YP 6610	B		1126	YR 3818	AK		34	PB 9562		
1107	YP 6621	P		1127	TA 1004	P		66	PB 1509		
1108	YP 6623	AH		1128	TA 1005	AE					
1109	YP 6624	D		1129	TA 1006	AE					
1110	YP 6625	A		1130	TA 1168	AE					
1111	YP 6632	W		1131	TA 1169	P					
1112	YP 6633	J		1132	TA 1170	AM					

A line up of AEC K type double deckers inside Swanley garage which opened in October 1925. The 401 Bexleyheath to Sevenoaks and 407 Sidcup to Bromley Station were the only routes operated at its opening so the photo may have been taken shortly afterwards; XB 8403 was withdrawn in January 1930 which forms the end "time barrier" for the photo.

S	Reg No.	Garage	Remark	S	Reg No.	Garage	Remark	S	Reg No.	Garage	Remark
1	XC 8183	V	MET	62	XD 8360	R		123	XH 3330	D	
2	XC 8344	R	MET	63	XD 8361	R	MET	124	XH 3331	D	
3	XC 8342	R	MET	64	XD 8363	R		125	XH 3332	D	
4	XC 8340	R	MET	65	XD 8364	R		126	XH 3333	AD	
5	XC 8341	R	MET	66	XD 8371	R		127	XH 3334	D	
6	XC 8343	R	MET	67	XD 8365	R		128	XH 3335	D	
7	XC 8308	R	MET	68	XD 8367	R		129	XH 3353	D	
8	XC 8307	R	MET	69	XD 8368	R		130	XH 3336	D	
9	XC 8349	R		70	XD 8383	R	SMET	131	XH 3337	D	
10	XC 8266	R	MET	71	XD 8378	R		132	XH 3338	D	
11	XC 8348	R	MET	72	XD 8369	R		133	XH 3339	D	
12	XC 8345	R	MET	73	XD 8381	R		134	XH 3340	D	
13	XC 8346	R	MET	74	XD 8382	R		135	XH 3354	D	
14	XC 8347	R	MET	75	XD 8370	R		136	XH 3341	D	
15	XC 8309	R	MET	76	XD 8379	R		137	XH 3342	D	
16	XD 8341	R	MET	77	XD 8380	R		138	XH 3343	D	
17	XD 8313	AL	MET	78	XD 8384	R		139	XH 3344	D	
18	XD 8314	AL	MET	79	XD 8398	D		140	XH 3345	AD	
19	XD 8319	AL	MET	80	XD 8385	R		141	XH 3346	D	
20	XD 8316	AL	MET	81	XD 8386	R		142	XH 3347	D	
21	XD 8317	AL	MET	82	XD 8387	R		143	XH 3348	D	
22	XD 8315	AL	MET	83	XD 8388	R		144	XP 4188	B	
23	XD 8321	AL	MET	84	XD 8395	R		145	XH 3349	AD	
24	XD 8330	AL	MET	85	XD 8396	R		146	XH 3350	D	
25	XD 8318	AL	MET	86	XD 8389	R		147	XH 3355	AD	
26	XD 8345	AL		87	XD 8392	R		148	XH 3356	D	
27	XD 8327	AL	MET	88	XD 8390	R		149	XH 3351	D	
28	XD 8320	AL	MET	89	XD 8397	R		150	XH 3352	D	
29	XD 8329	AL		90	XD 8391	R		151	XH 3357	D	
30	XD 8322	AL	MET	91	XD 8393	R		152	XH 3358	AD	
31	XD 8333	AL		92	XD 8394	R		153	XH 3359	D	
32	XD 8338	V		93	XH 3301	R		154	XH 3360	AD	
33	XD 8331	AL	MET	94	XH 3318	D		155	XH 3388	AD	
34	XD 8328	AL		95	XH 3302	R		156	XH 3361	AD	
35	XD 8332	AL	MET	96	XH 3303	R		157	XH 3362	AD	
36	XD 8334	AL	MET	97	XH 3304	R		158	XH 3363	D	
37	XD 8337	AL		98	XH 3319	D		159	XH 3364	AD	
38	XD 8335	AL		99	XH 3316	D		160	XH 3366	D	
39	XD 8340	R	MET	100	XH 3305	R		161	XH 3367	AD	
40	XD 8339	R	MET	101	XH 3306	R		162	XH 3365	AD	
41	XD 8336	AL		102	XH 3307	R		163	XH 3368	AD	
42	XD 8346	R	MET	103	XH 3308	D		164	XH 3369	AD	
43	XD 8347	R	MET	104	XH 3309	R		165	XH 3379	AD	
44	XD 8359	R		105	XH 3312	R		166	XH 3372	AD	
45	XD 8342	R	MET	106	XH 3310	R		167	XH 3373	AD	
46	XD 8343	R	MET	107	XH 3313	D		168	XH 3370	AD	
47	XD 8344	AL		108	XH 3320	D		169	XH 3371	AD	
48	XD 8355	R	MET	109	XH 3321	D		170	XH 3374	AD	
49	XD 8351	R		110	XD 8399	D		171	XH 3375	AD	
50	XH 3311	D		111	XH 3317	D		172	XH 3380	AD	
51	XD 8352	R		112	XH 3315	D		173	XH 3376	AD	
52	XD 8356	R	MET	113	XH 3322	D		174	XH 3377	AD	
53	XD 8349	R	MET	114	XD 8400	D		175	XH 3378	AD	
54	XD 8348	R		115	XH 3314	D		176	XH 3381	AD	
55	XD 8350	R	MET	116	XH 3315	D		177	XH 3400	W	
56	XD 8353	R	MET	117	XH 3324	D		178	XH 3389	AD	
57	XD 8358	R	MET	118	XH 3325	D		179	XH 3382	AD	
58	XD 8357	R	MET	119	XH 3326	D		180	XH 3383	AD	
59	XD 8354	R	MET	120	XH 3327	D		181	XH 3384	AD	
60	XD 8362	R	MET	121	XH 3328	D		182	XH 5919	W	
61	XD 8366	R		122	XH 3329	D		183	XH 3390	W	

S	Reg No.	Garage	Remark	S	Reg No.	Garage	Remark	S	Reg. No.	Garage	Remark
184	XH 3385	AD		245	XH 5945	T		306	XL 3721	J	
185	XH 3391	W		246	XH 5946	T		307	XL 3729	J	
186	XH 3386	AD		247	XH 5947	T		308	XL 3722	J	
187	XH 3392	W		248	XH 5948	W	MET	309	XL 3723	J	
188	XH 3387	AD		249	XH 5949	T		310	XL 3724	J	
189	XH 3393	W		250	XH 5967	W	MET	311	XL 3725	J	
190	XH 3394	W		251	XH 5950	W		312	XL 3730	J	
191	XH 3395	AD		252	XH 5973	V	MET	313	XL 3726	J	
192	XH 3396	W		253	XH 5951	W		314	XL 3727	J	
193	XH 3397	W		254	XH 5954	W	MET	315	XL 3728	J	
194	XH 3398	W		255	XH 5974	V	MET	316	XL 3731	J	
195	XH 3399	W		256	XH 5952	W	MET	317	XL 3732	J	
196	XH 5901	AD		257	XH 5955	W	MET	318	XL 3733	J	
197	XH 5902	AD		258	XH 5964	W	MET	319	XL 3734	J	
198	XH 5903	W		259	XH 5956	W	MET	320	XL 3735	J	
199	XH 5904	T		260	XH 5953	W		321	XL 3736	J	
200	XH 5905	W		261	XH 5962	W	MET	322	XL 3737	J	
201	XH 5907	W		262	XH 5965	V	MET	323	XL 3738	J	
202	XH 5908	T		263	XH 5966	V	MET	324	XL 3752	F	
203	XH 2906	W		264	XH 5975	W	MET	325	XL 3719	F	
204	XH 2909	W		265	XH 5978	K	S32	326	XL 3739	F	
205	XH 5910	T		266	XH 6000	G	MET	327	NK 4473		NAT
206	XH 5911	W		267	XH 5982	W		328	XL 3741	J	
207	XH 5912	W		268	XH 5983	W		329	XL 3742	J	
208	XH 5913	T		269	XH 5984	W		330	XL 3743	F	
209	XH 5914	T		270	XH 5985	W		331	NK 4189		NAT
210	XH 5915	W		271	XH 5986	W		332	XL 3745	F	
211	XH 5916	T		272	XH 5987	G	MET	333	XL 3746	F	
212	XH 5917	W		273	XH 5988	G	MET	334	XL 3747	F	
213	XH 5923	W		274	XH 5989	G		335	XL 3753	F	
214	XH 2918	W		275	XH 5990	G	MET	336	XL 3748	F	
215	XH 5620	W		276	XH 5991	G		337	XL 3749	F	
216	XH 5960	W	MET	277	XH 5992	G	MET	338	XL 3750	F	
217	XH 5921	W		278	XH 5993	G	MET	339	XL 3751	F	
218	XH 5963	W	MET	279	XH 5994	G	MET	340	XL 3754	F	
219	XH 5961	W	MET	280	XH 5995	G		341	XL 3755	F	
220	XH 5957	W	MET	281	XH 5996	G	MET	342	XL 3756	F	
221	XH 5922	W		282	XH 5997	G	MET	343	XL 3757	F	
222	XH 5929	W		283	XH 5998	G	MET	344	XL 3758	F	
223	XH 5958	W	MET	284	XH 5999	G	MET	345	XL 3759	F	
224	XH 5924	W		285	XL 3701	G		346	XL 3760	F	
225	XH 5934	T		286	XL 3702	AL		347	XL 3761	F	
226	XH 5925	W		287	XL 3703	AL		348	XL 3772	B	
227	XH 5926	W		288	XL 3704	AL		349	XL 3740	F	
228	XH 5927	W		289	XL 3705	AL		350	XL 3775	F	
229	XH 5928	W		290	XL 3706	AL		351	XL 3762	J	
230	XH 5930	T		291	XL 3707	AL		352	XL 3763	F	
231	XH 5940	W	MET	292	XL 3708	AL		353	XL 3764	F	
232	XH 5935	T		293	XL 3709	AL		354	NK 4188		NAT
233	XH 5936	T		294	XL 3744	F		355	XL 3776	B	
234	XH 5931	W		295	XL 3710	AL		356	XL 3766	F	
235	XH 5932	W		296	XL 3711	AL		357	XL 3767	F	
236	XH 5959	W	MET	297	XL 3712	AL		358	XL 3768	F	
237	XH 5937	T		298	XL 3713	AL		359	XL 3773	B	
238	XH 5933	D		299	XL 3714	AL		360	XL 3769	F	
239	XH 5938	T		300	XL 3715	AL		361	XL 3770	F	
240	XH 5941	T		301	XL 3716	W		362	XL 3777	B	
241	XH 5939	T		302	XL 3717	J		363	XL 3774	B	
242	XH 5942	T		303	NK 4115		NAT	364	XL 3765	F	
243	XH 5943	T		304	XL 3718	J		365	XL 3778	B	
244	XH 5944	T		305	XL 3720	J		366	XL 3799	B	

S	Reg. No.	Garage	Remark	S	Reg. No.	Garage	Remark	S	Reg. No.	Garage	Remark
367	XL 3788	B		428	XL 8936	T		489	XL 8997	X	
368	XL 8922	P		429	XL 8937	X		490	XM 720	X	
369	XL 3779	K	S30	430	XL 8938	J		491	XL 8999	X	
370	XL 3782	R		431	XL 8939	J		492	XL 9000	G	
371	XL 3780	K	S30	432	XL 8950	B		493	XM 701	G	
372	XL 3781	D		433	XL 8940	AK	S30	494	XL 702	G	
373	XL 3785	B		434	XL 8941	AH		495	XL 703	G	
374	XL 3783	J		435	XL 8942	T		496	XL 704	G	
375	XL 3784	D		436	XL 8943	T		497	XL 705	G	
376	XL 8904	J		437	XL 8951	J		498	XL 706	G	
377	XL 3800	E	S30	438	XL 8944	J		499	XL 708	G	
378	XL 3786	D		439	XL 8945	AK	S30	500	XL 707	G	
379	XL 3789	C	S30	440	XL 8946	J		501	XL 709	G	
380	XL 3790	B		441	XL 8947	G		502	XL 785	AL	
381	XL 3787	R		442	XL 8948	AK	S30	503	XL 711	G	
382	XL 3791	E	S30	443	XL 8987	X		504	XL 726	G	
383	XL 8908	F		444	XL 8952	T		505	XL 712	G	
384	XL 3792	E	S30	445	XL 8953	AH		506	XL 713	G	
385	XL 3793	B		446	XL 8954	AH		507	XL 714	G	
386	XL 3794	C	S30	447	XL 8955	K	S30	508	XL 753	G	
387	NK 4286		NAT	448	XL 8956	AH		509	XL 715	G	
388	NK 4287		NAT	449	XL 8957	AH		510	XL 716	G	
389	NK 4335		NAT	450	XL 8958	AH		511	XL 717	G	
390	NK 4474		NAT	451	XL 8959	AH		512	XL 718	K	S30
391	XL 3798	C	S30	452	XL 8960	AH		513	XL 719	G	
392	XL 8905	J		453	XL 8961	AH		514	XL 721	G	
393	XL 8902	B		454	XL 8962	AH		515	XL 722	G	
394	XL 8909	J		455	XL 8963	AH		516	XL 723	K	S30
395	XL 8903	B		456	XL 8964	AH		517	XL 724	G	
396	XL 8906	J		457	XL 8965	AH		518	XL 725	G	
397	XL 8910	F		458	XM 710	K	S30	519	XL 737	G	
398	XL 8914	Q		459	XL 8966	AH		520	XL 727	G	
399	XL 8907	F		460	XL 8967	G		521	XL 739	G	
400	XL 8911	F		461	XL 8968	X		522	XM 728	G	
401	XL 8912	F		462	XL 8969	G		523	XM 729	G	
402	XL 8913	F		463	XL 8970	X		524	XM 730	K	S30
403	XL 8915	Q		464	XL 8971	AH		525	XM 731	G	
404	XL 8916	Q		465	XL 8972	AH		526	XM 732	G	
405	XL 8917	Q		466	XL 8995	G		527	XM 733	G	
406	XL 8918	Q		467	XL 8973	G		528	XM 734	G	
407	XL 8919	P		468	XL 8974	X		529	XM 735	G	
408	XL 8920	C	S30	469	XL 8975	X		530	XM 736	G	
409	XL 8921	C	S30	470	XL 8976	X		531	XM 738	K	S30
410	XL 8926	P		471	XL 8977	X		532	XM 2409	Q	
411	XL 8923	P		472	XL 8978	L	S30	533	XM 740	G	
412	XL 8929	P		473	XL 8979	G		534	XM 741	G	
413	XL 8927	P		474	XL 8980	X		535	XM 742	P	
414	XL 8924	P		475	XL 8981	X		536	XM 743	P	
415	XL 8925	P		476	XL 8982	X		537	XM 744	P	
416	XL 8928	P		477	XL 8983	X		538	XM 745	AD	
417	XL 3795	C	S30	478	XL 8984	X		539	XM 746	P	
418	XL 8930	T		479	XL 8985	G		540	XM 747	P	
419	XL 3796	P		480	XL 8986	X		541	XM 754	P	
420	XL 8931	P		481	XL 8988	X		512	XM 748	P	
421	XL 8932	T		482	XL 8989	X		543	XM 749	P	
422	XL 8949	T		483	XL 8990	X		544	XM 750	P	
423	XL 8933	C	S30	484	XL 8991	X		545	XM 751	P	
424	XL 3793	C	S30	485	XL 8992	X		546	XM 766	CF	
425	XL 8934	C	S30	486	XL 8993	X		547	XM 755	AD	
426	XL 8901	P		487	XL 8994	X		548	XM 767	CF	
427	XL 8935	J		488	XL 8996	X		549	XM 756	AD	

111

S	Reg No.	Garage	Remark	S	Reg No.	Garage	Remark	S	Reg No.	Garage	Remark
550	XM 757	P		611	XM 2419	P		672	XM 2474	AK	
551	XM 768	CF		612	XM 2434	B		673	XM 2475	AK	
552	XM 758	P		613	XM 2420	N		674	XM 2476	M	
553	XM 752	P		614	XM 2421	N		675	XM 2477	M	
554	XM 781	AL		645	XM 2425	B		676	XM 2478	AK	
555	XM 759	AD		616	XM 2423	AK		677	XM 2479	AD	
556	XM 760	CF		617	XM 2412	AK		678	XM 2480	AK	
557	XM 761	AD		618	XM 2426	AK		679	XN 1717	R	
558	XM 769	AD		619	XM 2428	AK		680	XM 2481	G	
559	XM 777	AL		620	XM 2429	N		681	XM 2494	AD	
560	XM 762	CF		621	XM 2430	·N		682	XM 2483	AR	
561	XM 763	CF		622	XM 2413	B		683	XM 2484	AP	
562	XM 764	AD		623	XM 2435	G		684	XN 1711	AP	
563	XM 765	AD		624	XM 2414	B		685	XM 2485	M	
564	XM 2427	N		625	XM 2432	N		686	XM 2486	G	
565	XM 770	P		626	XM 2433	G		687	XM 2487	AK	
566	XM 771	CF		627	XM 2437	N		688	XM 2488	AD	
567	XM 772	CF		628	XM 2438	G		689	XM 2489	M	
568	XM 774	CF		629	XM 2439	N		690	XM 2490	AR	
569	XM 773	CF	MET	630	XM 2440	N		691	XM 2491	AR	
570	XM 775	AL		631	XM 2441	G		692	XM 2492	G	
571	XM 778	AL		632	XM 2442	G		693	XM 2495	AR	
572	XM 776	AL		633	XM 2443	G		694	XM 2496	AK	
573	XM 786	AL		634	XM 2444	U		695	XM 2497	AJ	
574	XM 779	AL		635	XM 2445	G		696	XM 2498	AD	
575	XM 787	AL		636	XM 2446	G		697	XM 2499	AR	
576	XM 788	SL		637	XM 2447	G		698	XM 2500	AK	
577	XM 780	AL		638	XM 2448	G		699	XM 7301	AK	
578	XM 791	N		639	XM 2449	G		700	XM 7348	AP	
579	XM 782	AL		640	XM 2450	G		701	XN 1716	AR	
580	XM 783	AL		641	XM 2451	G		702	XM 7302	AK	
581	XM 784	AL		642	XH 5979	W		703	XM 7365	AP	
582	XM 789	N		643	XH 5980	W		704	XM 7303	AP	
583	XM 792	P		644	XH 5981	W		705	XM 7304	AK	
584	XM 2436	N		645	XL 5771	B		706	XM 7305	AK	
585	XM 795	Q		646	XM 7341	AP		707	XM 7306	AK	
586	XM 790	AL		647	XM 2453	G		708	XM 7307	AD	
587	XM 793	N		648	XM 2454	AK		709	XM 7308	AR	
588	XM 796	Q		649	XM 2455	G		710	XM 7309	AR	
589	XM 794	N		650	XM 2463	AR		711	XM 7310	AR	
590	XM 797	N		651	XM 2456	AK		712	XM 7311	AP	
591	XM 2401	Q		652	XM 2464	M		713	XM 7312	G	
592	XM 2424	N		653	XM 2457	G		714	XM 7313	AR	
593	XM 798	Q		654	XM 2458	G		715	XM 7314	AK	
594	XM 2431	N		655	XM 2468	AK		716	XM 7315	G	
595	XM 799	Q		656	XN 1725	R		717	XM 7316	G	
596	XM 2402	Q		657	XM 2467	AR		718	XM 7317	AP	
597	XM 800	Q		658	XM 2462	G		719	XM 7349	AR	
598	XM 2403	Q		659	XM 2459	G		720	XM 7318	AP	
599	XM 2422	N		660	XM 2460	G		721	XM 7319	AP	
600	XM 2404	Q		661	XM 2461	G		722	XM 7320	AR	
601	XM 2405	Q		662	XM 2465	G		723	XM 7321	AK	
602	XM 2408	Q		663	XM 2466	AK		724	XM 7322	G	
603	XM 2406	Q		664	XM 2452	M		725	XM 7323	AP	
604	XM 2407	Q		665	XM 2482	M		726	XM 7324	AR	
605	XM 2416	P		666	XM 2469	AK		727	XN 1723	B	
606	XM 2410	Q		667	XM 2470	AK		728	XM 7325	AK	
607	XM 2411	Q		668	XM 2471	AK		729	XM 7350	AP	
608	XM 2417	P		669	XM 2472	AK		730	XM 7326	AR	
609	XM 2418	P		670	XM 2493	AK		731	XN 1726	AR	
610	XM 2415	P		671	XM 2473	AK		732	XM 7327	AK	

S	Reg No.	Garage	Remark	S	Reg No.	Garage	Remark	S	Reg No.	Garage	Remark
733	XM 7366	AP		794	XM 7363	AP		853	XN 1709	R	
734	XN 1732	AR		795	XM 7375	AP		854	XN 1710	R	
735	XN 1761	AD		796	XM 7376	AP		855	NK 5802		NAT
736	XN 1731	M		797	XM 7377	AP		856	XN 1701	M	
737	XM 7328	AR		798	XN 1706	M		857	XN 1703	M	
738	XM 7329	AR		799	XN 1713	M		858	XO 4610	AL	S30
739	XM 7330	AR		800	XM 7362	AP		859	NK 5735		NAT
740	XM 7351	AR		801	XN 1714	AP		860	XN 1724	AD	
741	XN 1763	P		802	XN 1733	M		861	XO 4072	C	S30
742	XM 7399	AR		803	XN 1719	AD		862	XN 7046	P	
743	XM 7389	R		804	XM 7364	AP		863	XN 1751	AR	
744	XM 7352	AP		805	XM 7378	AP		864	XN 1742	M	
745	XN 1727	R		806	XM 7379	AP		865	NK 5801		NAT
746	XM 7331	AP		807	XN 1744	H		866	XO 7611	AK	S30
747	XN 1760	AD		808	XM 7380	AP		867	XN 1752	AR	
748	XN 1722	AD		809	XN 7043	P		868	XN 1753	AR	
749	XM 7332	AR		810	XN 1746	G		869	XN 1754	AR	
750	XM 7342	AR		811	XN 7381	B		870	XN 1762	AD	
751	XM 7353	AP		812	XN 7382	AP		871	XN 1755	AR	
752	XM 7354	AR		813	XN 1735	M		872	XO 7612	AK	S30
753	XN 1736	M		814	XM 7383	AP		873	XO 4088	C	S30
754	XM 7333	AK		815	XM 7391	AP		874	XN 1739	M	
755	XM 7334	AR		816	XM 7384	AP		875	XO 7613	AK	S30
756	XM 7367	AP		817	XM 7385	AP		876	XN 1777	AD	
757	XN 1702	M		818	XM 7386	AP		877	XO 7614	K	S30
758	XM 7335	AP		819	XM 7387	AP		878	XO 4073	C	S30
759	XM 7336	AP		820	XN 7050	P		879	XN 1740	AR	
760	XM 7343	AR		821	XM 7388	B		880	XN 1741	M	
761	XM 7368	AP		822	XO 4067	C	S30	881	XO 4079	K	S30
762	XM 7337	AR		823	XN 1759	G		882	XN 1779	C	S30
763	XN 7355 ✗	AP		824	XN 1728	M		883	XO 4080	L	
764	XM 7338	AK		825	XN 7044	P		884	XO 4089	C	S30
765	XM 7344	~~AR~~		826	XN 7045	P		885	XN 1756	G	
766	XM 7355 ✗	AP 7356(?)		827	XN 1738	M		886	XN 1715	AP	
767	XN 1718	R		828	XM 7392	AP		887	XO 4095	C	S30
768	XM 7357	AP		829	XN 1720	B		888	XN 1730	M	
769	XM 7358	AP		830	XM 7393	R		889	XN 1765	C	S30
770	XM 7339	AR		831	XM 7394	B		890	XN 1757	C	S30
771	XN 1734	M		832	XN 1758	AR		891	XN 1729	R	
772	XM 7340	AK		833	XN 1782	C	S30	892	XN 1781	C	S30
773	XM 7359	AP		834	XN 1747	AK		893	XN 1764	C	S30
774	XM 7345	AR		835	PD 5983		ESTC S30	894	XO 4051	L	
775	XM 7346	AP		836	XN 1783	C	S30	895	XO 4081	L	
776	XO 4096	AK	S30	837	XN 1748	AD		896	XR 9985	D	Ex Ch.
777	XM 7369	AP		838	XO 4050	N		897	XO 9229	AR	
778	XM 7390	AP		839	NK 5736		NAT	898	XO 9230	AR	
779	XM 7347	AR		840	XM 7395	AP		899	XO 9231	AR	
780	XO 4097	AK	S30	841	PD 5981		ESTC S30	900	?		
781	XM 7370	AP		842	XO 7609	C	S30	901	NK 7365		NAT
782	XM 7360	AP		843	XM 7396	AP		902	XU 6193	T	
783	XN 1743	P		844	XO 4018	AH		903	YR 3876	W	
784	XM 7371	AR		845	XN 1750	AR		904	YR 3877		NAT
785	XN 1737	AR		846	XN 1749	AR		905	YR 3881	W	
786	XN 1721	B		847	XM 7397	AP		906	YR 3884		NAT
787	XN 1704	AP		848	XN 1771	AD		907	YR 3882	W	
788	XM 7361	AP		849	XM 7398	M		908	YR 3885		NAT
789	XM 7372	R		850	XN 1707	AP		909	YR 3887	V	
790	XN 1705	R		851	XN 1708	AD		910	YR 3886		NAT
791	XM 7373	M		852	XN 1772	C	S30	911	YR 3888	W	
792	XM 7374	AP						912	YR 3889	W	
793	XN 1712	AP						913	YR 3891	W	

(handwritten note near 857–858: "(4064)?" with arrow pointing to XO 4610)

113

S	Reg No.	Garage	Remark
914	YR 3883	W	
915	YH 1101		NAT
916	YH 1102		NAT
917	YH 1103		NAT
918	YH 1104		NAT
919	YH 1105		NAT
920	YH 1106		NAT
921	YH 1107		NAT
922	YH 1108		NAT
923	YH 1109		NAT
924	YH 1110		NAT
925	YH 1111		NAT
926	YH 1112		NAT
927	YH 1113		NAT
928	YT 4898	AL	Ex Tv.

PS TYPE
NATIONAL

PS	Reg No.	Garage	Remark
1	NK 5581		
2	NK 5582		
3	NK 5583		
4	XN 1800		
5	NK 6001		
6	NK 6002		
7	NK 6003		

PS	Reg No.	Garage	Remark
8	NK 6088		
9	NK 6089		
10	NK 6090		
11	NK 6123		
12	NK 6124		
13	NK 6144		
14	RO 2974		
15	RO 2975		

EAST SURREY

PS	Reg No.	Garage	Remark
119	PD 9752		
114	PD 9753		
127	PD 9754		
116	PD 9755		
126	PD 9756		
124	PD 1348		
123	PD 1349		
125	PD 1350		
179	PD 1351		
117	PD 1352		
128	PD 1353		
112	PD 1354		
115	PD 1355		
118	PD 1356		
121	PD 1357		
130	PD 1358		
172	PD 1359		

PS	Reg No.	Garage	Remark
113	PD 1360		
120	PD 1361		
131	PD 1362		
132	PD 1363		
137	PD 1364		
136	PD 1365		
135	PD 1366		
134	PD 1367		
138	PD 1368		
142	PD 1369		
140	PD 1370		
141	PD 1371		
139	PD 1372		
144	PE 8309		
143	PE 8310		
147	PE 8311		
148	PE 8312		
145	PE 8313		
146	PE 8314		
168	PF 9016		
169	PF 9017		
170	PF 9018		
171	PF 9019		
172	PF 9020		
173	PF 9021		
174	PF 9022		
175	PF 9023		

S265 the prototype single decker version is seen at Kingston in April 1922 working on the long 115 route to Guildford. It was transferred to the "National" fleet north of the LGOC area, in September 1922. (London Transport U38471)

NS	Reg No.	Garage	Remark	NS	Reg No.	Garage	Remark	NS	Reg No.	Garage	Remark
1	XO 1019	AD		62	XN 7096	M		123	XN 7061	AD	
2	XR 1442	AE		63	XN 7019	R		124	XN 7088	D	
3	XO 9273	AP		64	XN 7041	M		125	XN 7068	AR	
4	XO 9268	AP		65	XN 7020	R		126	XO 1036	M	
5	XN 7005	R		66	XN 7033	M		127	XN 7074	AR	
6	XN 1799	R		67	XN 7034	M		128	XO 1013	D	
7	XN 1776	R		68	XN 7021	R		129	XN 7089	AR	
8	XN 1796	R		69	XN 7062	AR		130	XO 1037	M	
9	XN 1780	R		70	XN 1086	D		131	XN 7090	D	MET
10	XN 1791	R		71	XN 7047	R	MET	132	XO 1007	AP	
11	XO 1004	M		72	XN 7022	R		133	XN 7082	AR	
12	XN 1792	R	MET	73	XN 7035	M		134	XN 7085	D	
13	XN 1786	R		74	XN 7042	AR		135	XN 7083	D	
14	XN 7006	R		75	XN 7027	R		136	XO 1014	AP	
15	XN 1787	R		76	XN 7023	R		137	XO 1015	AD	
16	XN 1784	M		77	XO 1020	M		138	XO 1008	AD	MET
17	XN 1793	R	MET	78	XN 7063	AR		139	XN 7076	AR	
18	XN 1788	R		79	XN 7056	M		140	XO 1060	R	
19	XN 1794	R	MET	80	XN 7040	AR		141	XN 7077	AR	
20	XN 1789	R		81	XN 7052	M		142	XN 7099	D	
21	XN 1797	R		82	XN 7036	D		143	XN 7091	D	
22	XN 1790	R		83	XN 7037	M		144	XO 1038	M	
23	XN 1795	R		84	XN 7024	R		145	XN 7078	D	
24	XN 1767	R	MET	85	XN 7025	M		146	XO 1021	M	
25	XN 1745	R		86	XN 7079	D		147	XN 7092	D	
26	XN 1798	R		87	XN 7081	AR		148	XO 1039	M	
27	XN 1773	R		88	XN 7038	AR		149	XN 7093	D	
28	XN 1770	R		89	XN 7053	M		150	XO 1061	M	
29	XN 1766	AR		90	XN 7064	AR		150	XO 1022	D	
30	XN 7007	R		91	XN 7054	AR		152	XO 1062	M	
31	XN 1774	M		92	XN 7048	M		153	XO 1095	AD	
32	XN 1778	R		93	XN 7098	D		154	XO 1055	AD	
33	XN 1769	R		94	XN 7069	AR		155	XO 1016	D	
34	XN 7008	M		95	XN 7070	AR		156	XN 7084	N	
35	XN 7080	AR		96	XN 7075	M		157	XO 1023	M	
36	XN 1775	M		97	XN 7094	D		158	XO 1017	D	
37	XN 7051	M		98	XN 7071	AR	MET	159	XO 1031	M	
38	XO 1028	M		99	XN 7057	D		160	XO 1054	AP	
39	XN 1785	AR		100	XN 7055	M		161	XO 1009	M	
40	XN 7009	R		101	XN 7049	M		162	XO 1078	AD	
41	XN 7010	R		102	XO 1001	AR		163	XO 1032	M	
42	XN 1768	D		103	XN 7065	D		164	XO 1024	M	
43	XN 7028	R		104	XN 7066	AR		165	XO 1033	AD	
44	XN 7001	AR		105	XN 7058	AR		166	XO 1010	D	
45	XN 7030	M		106	XN 7100	M		167	XO 1063	M	
46	XN 7029	M		107	XN 7095	M		168	XO 1025	M	
47	XN 7026	R		108	XN 7072	B		169	XO 1056	AD	
48	XN 7011	R		109	XO 1002	D		170	XO 1018	M	
49	XN 7012	R		110	XN 7087	M		171	XO 1034	M	
50	XN 7013	R		111	XN 7097	D		172	XO 1096	AR	
51	XN 7014	R		112	XN 7059	AR		173	XO 1026	M	
52	XN 7015	R		113	XO 1003	D		174	XO 1048	R	
53	XN 7002	R		114	XN 7067	AR		175	XO 1049	AD	
54	XN 7031	R		115	XO 1005	AD		176	XO 1040	AD	
55	XN 7016	R		116	XO 1046	M		177	XO 1050	M	
56	XN 7003	R		117	XO 1030	M		178	XO 1071	AD	
57	XN 7017	R		118	XN 7060	AR		179	XO 1011	D	
58	XN 7004	R	MET	119	XN 7073	AR		180	XO 1027	M	
59	XN 7039	M		120	XO 1047	M		181	XO 1097	AD	
60	XN 7032	M		121	XO 1006	D		182	XO 1064	R	
61	XN 7018	R		122	XO 1012	D		183	XO 1072	M	

NS	Reg No.	Garage	Remark	NS	Reg No.	Garage	Remark	NS	Reg No.	Garage	Remark
184	XO 1057	M		245	XO 1114	AD		306	XO 1181	CF	
185	XO 1079	AD		246	XO 1117	AR		307	XO 1176	B	
186	XO 1035	M		247	XO 1127	AD		308	XO 1175	AP	
187	XO 1065	AD		248	XO 1132	AD		309	XO 1182	AP	
188	XO 1066	M		249	XO 1109	AD		310	XO 1166	AR	
189	XO 1051	M		250	XO 1083	AD		311	XO 1183	B	
190	XO 1029	M		251	XO 1142	AD		312	XO 1174	AP	
191	XO 1052	R		252	XO 1133	AR		313	XO 1172	AP	
192	XO 1041	M		253	XO 1118	AD		314	XO 1184	B	
193	XO 1042	M		254	XO 1128	AR		315	XO 1185	CF	
194	XO 1053	M		255	XO 1138	AD		316	XO 1186	AP	
195	XO 1043	M		256	XO 1124	AD		317	XO 1187	CF	
196	XO 1067	M		257	XO 1129	AD		318	XO 1188	CF	
197	XO 1044	M		258	XO 1134	AR		319	XO 1169	AR	
198	XO 1098	R		259	XO 1130	B	MET	320	XO 1189	CF	
199	XO 1045	AD		260	XO 1140	AR		321	XO 1190	B	
200	XO 1080	AD		261	XO 1131	AD		322	XO 4005	AP	
201	XO 1073	AD		262	XO 1143	AD		323	XO 1195	CF	
202	XO 1068	M		263	XO 1115	AD		324	XO 1200	AD	
203	XO 1081	AD		264	XO 1135	AD		325	XO 1196	AD	
204	XO 1058	N		265	XO 1144	AD		326	XO 1191	CF	
205	XO 1088	AD	MET	266	XO 1141	AD		327	XO 1197	G	
206	XO 1069	M		267	XO 1136	AP		328	XO 4085	B	
207	XO 1099	R		268	XO 1145	AD		329	XO 4003	AP	
208	XO 1070	M		269	XO 1146	AD		330	XO 4004	AP	
209	XO 1086	AD		270	XO 1153	AR		331	XO 1192	AR	MET
210	XO 1074	AD		271	XO 1154	AR		332	XO 4007	G	
211	XO 1059	AD		272	XO 1147	AD		333	XO 1198	AP	
212	XO 1084	R		273	XO 1152	AD		334	XO 4008	AP	
213	XO 1085	AD		274	XO 1148	AD		335	XO 4009	AP	
214	XO 1106	R		275	XO 1155	AR		336	XO 4028	AP	
215	XO 1108	R		276	XO 1119	AD		337	XO 4002	AP	MET
216	XO 1087	AD		277	XO 1137	AR		338	XO 1199	CF	
217	XO 1075	R		278	XO 1156	AP		339	XO 4010	G	MET
218	XO 1076	M		279	XO 1157	AR		340	XO 4029	AP	
219	XO 1077	R		280	XO 1158	AR	MET	341	XO 4011	AP	
220	XO 1125	AD		281	XO 1159	AR		342	XO 4093	AP	
221	XO 1100	AD		282	XO 1149	AR		343	XO 4019	R	
222	XO 1107	AD		283	XO 1160	AR		344	XO 4030	AP	
223	XO 1089	R		284	XO 1171	AP	MET	345	XO 4012	AP	
224	XO 1111	AD		285	XO 1177	B		346	XO 4020	AP	
225	XO 1090	R	MET	286	XO 1161	AR		347	XO 4031	AP	
226	XO 1091	AD		287	XO 1193	G		378	XO 4021	AP	
227	XO 1112	AD		288	XO 1150	AD		379	XO 4013	AP	
228	XO 1110	R		289	XO 1139	AD		350	XO 4014	AP	
229	XO 1092	AD		290	XO 1167	AR		351	XO 4053	R	
230	XO 1093	R		291	XO 1168	G		352	XO 4022	G	MET
231	XO 1103	AD		292	XO 1162	AR		353	XO 4032	R	
232	XO 1101	M		293	XO 1178	B		354	XO 4015	AP	
233	XO 1094	AD		294	XO 1151	AD		355	XO 4033	AP	
234	XO 1120	AD		295	XO 1163	AR		356	XO 4023	AP	
235	XO 1102	AR		296	XO 1179	B		357	XO 4016	AP	
236	XO 1121	AD		297	XO 4001	G		358	XO 4068	G	
237	XO 1104	AD		298	XO 4026	R		359	XO 4017	AP	
238	XO 1122	AR		299	XO 1164	AR		360	XO 4024	AP	
239	XO 1126	AD		300	XO 1194	CF		361	XO 4069	R	
240	XO 1116	AD	MET	301	XO 1170	AR	MET	362	XO 4034	AP	
241	XO 1105	M		302	XO 4027	AP		363	XO 4025	AP	
242	XO 1123	AD		303	XO 1173	B		364	XO 4064	G	
423	XO 1082	M		304	XO 1165	AR		365	XO 4006	AP	
244	XO 1113	AD		305	XO 1180	B		366	XO 4052	R	

NS	Reg No.	Garage	Remark	NS	Reg No.	Garage	Remark	NS	Reg. No.	Garage	Remark
367	XO 4035	AP		428	XO 4058	R		489	XO 7659	E	
368	XO 7605	AP		429	XO 4078	R		490	XO 9210	E	
369	XO 4082	R		430	XO 7681	E		491	XO 7638	AP	
370	XO 4038	R		431	XO 7666	N		492	XO 7686	N	
371	XO 4054	AP		432	XO 7682	E		493	XO 7687	E	
372	XO 4074	G		433	XO 7627	AP		494	XO 7673	E	
373	XO 4036	AP		434	XO 4083	G		495	XO 7640	E	
374	XO 4056	G		435	XO 7608	AP		496	XO 7662	G	
375	XO 4039	G		436	XO 7653	E		497	XO 9204	CF	
376	XO 4063	AP		437	XO 7622	AP		498	XO 9232	AL	
377	XO 7606	AP		438	XO 4091	B		499	XO 7674	E	
378	XO 4060	AP		439	XO 4086	B		500	XO 7675	E	
379	XO 4061	R		440	XO 7615	AP		501	XO 7688	E	
380	XO 4059	AP		441	XO 7670	E		502	XO 7632	AP	
381	XO 4040	R		442	XO 7657	E		503	XO 7633	E	MET
382	XO 7616	E		443	XO 7655	E		504	XO 7644	AP	
383	XO 4041	AP		444	XO 4087	G		505	XO 7648	AP	
384	XO 4042	R		445	XO 4099	AP		506	XO 7645	AP	
385	XO 9249	X		446	XO 7656	E		507	XO 7689	E	
386	XO 9243	CF		447	XO 4094	AP		508	XO 7690	E	
387	XO 9254	AP		448	XO 7624	AP		509	XO 7676	AL	
388	XO 9248	J		449	XO 7664	G		510	XO 9270	AP	
389	XO 9269	CF		450	XO 7607	AP		511	XO 7691	E	
390	XO 9260	J		451	XO 7643	E		512	XO 7698	CF	
391	XO 9241	AL		452	XO 7661	G		513	XO 9222	CF	
392	XO 9263	J	MET	453	XO 7618	AP		514	XO 7646	E	
393	XO 4037	AL		454	XO 7623	AP		515	XO 9218	AL	
394	XO 9259	AP		455	XO 7683	E		516	XO 7641	AP	
395	XO 9242	AL		456	XO 7671	E		517	XO 9223	AL	
396	XO 9255	F		457	XO 7693	E	MET	518	XO 9265	AP	
397	XO 4055	AP		458	XO 7684	E		519	XO 7692	E	
398	XO 4066	R		459	XO 7668	E		520	XO 7677	E	MET
399	XO 4043	AP		460	XO 7625	AP		521	XO 9244	AL	
400	XO 7642	G	MET	461	XO 7617	AP		522	XO 7694	CF	
401	XO 7604	AP		462	XO 7700	CF		523	XO 7695	CF	
402	XO 4070	G		463	XO 7601	AP		524	XO 7696	E	
403	XO 7679	E		464	XO 7685	E		525	XO 9214	AL	
404	XO 7626	N		465	XO 7628	E		526	XO 9209	CF	
405	XO 4044	E		466	XO 7672	AL		527	XO 9219	CF	
406	XO 7651	G	MET	467	XO 7629	AP		528	XO 9233	CF	
407	XO 4071	G		468	XO 7649	E	MET	529	XO 9282	CF	MET
408	XO 4075	R		469	XO 7602	N		530	XO 7647	AP	
409	XO 7680	E		470	XO 7620	AP		531	XO 9234	AL	
410	XO 7639	G		471	XO 7634	AP		532	XO 9207	AL	
411	XO 4045	G		472	XO 9211	E		533	XO 9220	AL	
412	XO 4049	AP		473	XO 7669	AL		534	XO 9235	AL	
413	XO 4098	AP		474	XO 7619	AP		535	XO 7678	E	
414	XO 4046	R		475	XO 7658	E		536	XO 9236	AP	
415	XO 4047	AP		476	XO 7667	E		537	XO 9237	AL	
416	XO 4048	AP		477	XO 7635	E		538	XO 9215	CF	
417	XO 4076	R		478	XO 7630	AP		539	XO 9202	AL	
418	XO 4090	R		479	XO 7631	G		540	XO 9224	CF	
419	XO 4057	G		480	XO 9203	CF		541	XO 9251	X	
420	XO 4062	R		481	XO 7650	G		542	XO 9245	X	
421	XO 4077	B		482	XO 7663	G		543	XO 9213	AL	
422	XO 4092	R		483	XO 7603	G		544	XO 9283	CF	
423	XO 7652	E		484	XO 7636	AP		545	XO 9217	AL	
424	XO 7621	G		485	XO 7660	E		546	XO 9246	AL	
425	XO 4084	R		486	XO 7654	G		547	XO 9208	N	MET
426	XO 7665	E		487	XO 7699	V		548	XO 9205	CF	
427	XO 4065	G		488	XO 7637	AP		549	XO 9225	CF	

NS	Reg No.	Garage	Remark	NS	Reg No.	Garage	Remark	NS	Reg No.	Garage	Remark
550	XO 9226	AL		611	XP 707	J		672	XP 752	D	
551	XO 9238	CF		612	XP 712	J		673	XP 757	F	
552	XO 9257	N		613	XP 735	F		674	XP 773	P	
553	XO 9212	AL		614	XP 716	J		675	XP 766	P	
554	XO 9221	AL		615	XP 708	J		676	XP 792	J	
555	XO 9206	N	MET	616	XP 720	F		677	XP 758	J	
556	XO 9227	CF		617	XP 713	J		678	XP 753	H	
557	XO 9239	AL	MET	618	XP 717	J		679	XP 780	P	
558	XO 9216	AL		619	XP 721	F		680	XP 768	P	
559	XO 7697	V		620	XP 724	J		681	XP 774	J	
560	XO 9252	AP	MET	621	XP 722	J		662	XP 767	P	
561	XO 9271	AP		622	XP 736	F		683	XP 795	D	
562	XO 9284	CF	MET	623	XP 725	F		684	XP 778	P	
563	XO 9256	X		624	XP 714	J		685	XP 775	P	
564	XO 9261	X		625	XP 718	F		686	XP 776	P	
565	XO 9247	X		626	XP 740	F		687	XP 781	P	
566	XO 9264	X		627	XP 426	J		688	XP 793	J	
567	XO 9258	CF		628	XP 741	F		689	XP 790	J	
568	XO 9201	CF		629	XP 727	F		690	XP 782	D	
569	XO 9240	CF	MET	630	XP 715	J		691	XP 764	F	
570	XO 9253	AP		631	XP 728	F		692	XP 794	J	
571	XO 9262	X		632	XP 729	F		693	XP 765	P	
572	XO 9228	CF		633	XP 723	H		694	XP 796	F	
573	XO 9300	J	MET	634	XP 754	F		695	XP 791	F	
574	XP 701	N		635	XP 755	F		696	XP 763	F	
575	XO 9274	CF		636	XP 769	P		697	XP 2463	T	
576	XO 9250	X		637	XP 742	P		698	XP 2451	H	
577	XP 702	N		638	XP 759	D		699	XP 788	J	
578	XO 9267	AL		639	XP 743	P		700	XP 2466	F	
579	XO 9279	X		640	XP 738	F		701	XP 2467	F	
580	XO 9278	X		641	XP 730	F		702	XP 798	J	
581	XO 9266	X		642	XP 770	P		733	XP 797	H	
582	XP 703	J		643	XP 731	F		704	XP 2501	T	
583	XO 9272	X		644	XP 799	J		705	XP 2454	J	
584	XO 9291	N		645	XP 737	J		706	XP 2460	J	
585	XO 9285	CF		646	XP 744	F		707	XP 2452	H	
586	XP 704	N		647	XP 745	J		708	XP 800	D	
587	XO 9292	N		648	XP 732	F		709	XP 2461	T	
588	XO 9286	CF		649	XP 733	F		710	XP 2453	J	
589	XO 9287	CF		650	XP 739	F		711	XP 2462	J	
590	XO 9280	X		651	XP 784	P		712	XP 2478	T	
591	XP 705	N		652	XP 789	F		713	XP 2464	H	
592	XO 9293	N		653	XP 779	R		714	XP 2455	F	
593	XO 9281	CF	MET	654	XP 777	P		715	XP 2479	H	
594	XO 9288	CF		655	XP 760	J		716	XP 2484	H	
595	XO 9277	CF	MET	656	XP 746	D		717	XP 2480	H	
596	XP 709	J	MET	657	XP 771	D		718	XP 2456	H	
597	XO 9294	N		658	XP 761	J		719	XP 2468	F	
598	XO 9296	N		659	XP 747	F		720	XP 2469	F	
599	XO 9297	J		660	XP 756	F		721	XP 2470	F	
600	XO 9289	CF		661	XP 734	F		722	XP 2523	AC	
601	XP 719	F	MET	662	XP 748	J		723	XP 2471	H	
602	XO 9275	CF		663	XP 749	D		724	XP 2457	F	
603	XO 9276	CF		664	XP 772	P		725	XP 2465	H	
604	XO 9295	J		665	XP 783	J		726	XP 2458	J	
605	XO 706	J		666	XP 785	F		727	XP 2459	J	
606	XO 9290	N		667	XP 762	D		728	XP 2472	F	
607	XP 710	J		668	XP 750	D		729	XP 2473	F	
608	XP 711	J	MET	669	XP 786	P		730	XP 2502	J	
609	XO 9298	J		670	XP 787	P		731	XP 2481	F	
610	XO 9299	J		671	XP 751	F		732	XP 2474	J	

NS	Reg No.	Garage	Remark	NS	Reg No.	Garage	Remark	NS	Reg No.	Garage	Remark
733	XP 2498	L		794	XP 2511	J		855	XP 4143	D	
734	XP 2485	H		795	XP 2512	J		856	XP 4177	M	
735	XP 2539	T		796	XP 2521	T		857	XP 4189	AC	
736	XP 2475	F		797	XP 4119	L		858	XP 4167	R	MET
737	XP 2482	J		798	XP 2530	T		859	XP 4154	M	
738	XP 2483	J		799	XP 2547	AP		860	XP 4170	M	
739	XP 2497	J		800	XP 2522	T		861	XP 4190	M	
740	XP 2486	H		801	XP 2531	T		862	XP 4155	U	
741	XP 2492	X		802	XP 4138	AP		863	XP 4164	U	
742	XP 2493	H		803	XP 2532	L		864	XP 4191	R	
743	XP 2487	H		804	XP 4152	D		865	XP 4168	M	
744	XP 2491	H		805	XP 2548	T		866	XP 4192	U	
745	XP 2488	H		806	XP 2533	T		867	XP 4169	M	
746	XP 2489	H		807	XP 2549	T		868	XP 6680	R	
747	XP 2524	T		808	XP 4115	L		869	XP 4193	R	
748	XP 2494	R		809	XP 4133	AR		870	XP 4175	U	MET
749	XP 2477	F		810	XP 4120	AF		871	XP 6620	AC	
750	XP 2490	H		811	XP 2534	T		872	XP 4165	U	
781	XP 2495	H		812	XP 2535	AP		873	XP 4166	R	
752	XP 2499	H		813	XP 2536	T		874	XP 4171	M	
753	XP 2476	G		814	XP 2537	T		875	XP 4176	M	
754	XP 2503	J		815	XP 4107	L		876	XP 4172	U	
755	XP 4116	AC		816	XP 4121	AP		877	XP 4197	R	
756	XP 2516	T		817	XP 4122	L		878	XP 4183	R	
757	XP 2500	J		818	XP 2538	T		879	XP 4177	U	
758	XP 4159	D		819	XP 4108	T		880	XP 4205	R	
759	XP 2504	M		820	XP 4123	AF		881	XP 4206	AC	
760	XP 2525	T		821	XP 4124	L		882	XP 6657	D	
761	XP 2513	J		822	XP 4153	AC		883	XP 4173	R	
762	XP 2529	E		823	XP 4125	AP		884	XP 4184	R	
763	XP 2543	L		824	XP 4126	AF		885	XP 4178	U	
764	XP 2505	J		825	XP 4139	AP		886	XP 4185	U	
765	XP 4112	Y		826	XP 4135	AR		887	XP 4198	R	
766	XP 2496	J		827	XP 2541	T		888	XP 4179	U	MET
767	XP 2544	AF		828	XP 4127	L		889	XP 6681	U	
768	XP 4151	AC		829	XP 4128	L		890	XP 4186	R	
769	XP 4136	AP		830	XP 4140	AP		891	XP 4199	U	
770	XP 2526	T		831	XP 4129	AF		892	XP 6601	U	
771	XP 2542	T		832	XP 4109	H		893	XP 4180	U	
772	XP 2506	J		833	XP 4130	AP		894	XP 6631	AC	
773	XP 4160	AR		834	XP 4113	T		895	XP 4182	R	
774	XP 2507	T		835	XP 4131	AC		896	XP 4200	D	
775	XP 4161	D		836	XP 4147	AP		897	XP 6602	U	
776	XP 2517	AR		837	XP 4163	D		898	XP 6659	U	
777	XP 4137	AF		838	XP 4114	AR		899	XP 6632	U	
778	XP 2508	T		839	XP 4156	AP		900	XP 4194	AC	
779	XP 2545	L		840	XP 4132	D		901	XP 6603	AC	
780	XP 4117	D		841	XP 4148	AP		902	XP 4195	AC	
781	XP 2514	J		842	XP 4141	AF		903	XP 4187	M	
782	XP 2518	T		843	XP 4142	AC		904	XP 4196	AC	
783	XP 2515	H		844	XP 4149	AC		905	XP 4202	R	
784	XP 4118	L		845	XP 4150	D		906	XP 4201	R	
785	XP 2527	J		846	XP 4143	AC		907	XP 4203	U	MET
786	XP 2540	T		847	XP 4144	AP		908	XP 6604	AC	
787	XP 2528	T		848	XP 6641	AC		909	XP 4204	AC	
788	XP 2546	T		849	XP 4157	D		910	XP 6682	M	
789	XP 2509	AP		850	XP 4110	L		911	XP 6605	AC	
790	XP 4162	R		851	XP 4111	T		912	XP 6660	AC	
791	XP 2510	AP		852	XP 4158	D		913	XP 6623	D	
792	XP 2519	T		853	XP 4145	D		914	XP 6610	AC	
793	XP 2520	D		854	XP 4146	AP		915	XP 6606	AC	

NS	Reg No.	Garage	Remark
916	XP 6607	AC	
917	XP 6624	U	
918	XP 6661	R	
919	XP 6625	AC	
920	XP 6611	AC	
921	XP 6658	D	
922	XP 6608	AC	
923	XP 6612	AC	
924	XP 6626	AC	
925	XP 6621	AC	
926	XP 6613	AC	
927	XP 6683	AC	
928	XP 6638	D	
929	XP 6675	AC	MET
930	XP 6642	AC	
931	XP 6627	AC	
932	XP 6614	D	
933	XP 6619	D	
934	XP 6615	AC	
935	XP 6633	X	
936	XP 6609	D	
937	XP 6634	D	
938	XP 6616	AC	
939	XP 6617	AC	
940	XP 6650	AC	
941	XP 6622	D	
942	XP 6651	AC	
943	XP 6618	AC	
944	XP 6652	X	
945	XP 6639	AC	
946	XP 6643	X	
947	XP 6676	AC	
948	XP 6628	U	
949	XP 8238	Q	
950	XP 6629	U	
951	XP 6662	M	
952	XP 6644	U	MET
953	XP 6653	D	
954	XP 6630	AC	
955	XP 6654	D	
956	XP 6677	AC	
957	XP 8239	B	
958	XP 6635	AC	
959	XP 6636	D	
960	XP 6645	AC	
961	XP 6696	R	
962	XP 6637	AC	
963	XP 8279	B	
964	XP 6663	U	
965	XP 6646	X	
966	XP 6684	CF	
967	XP 8228	Q	
968	XP 6664	AD	MET
969	XP 6640	D	
970	XP 6647	AC	
971	XP 6648	AC	
972	XP 6665	AC	
973	XP 8210	B	
974	XP 6685	AC	
975	XP 6672	AC	
976	XP 6669	AC	

NS	Reg No.	Garage	Remark
977	XP 6655	D	
978	XP 6686	AC	
979	XP 6691	AC	
980	XP 6666	M	
981	XP 6667	AC	
982	XP 6687	AC	
983	XP 8206	M	
984	XP 6656	AD	
985	XP 6673	AC	
986	XP 8225	Q	MET
987	XP 6674	M	
988	XP 6688	AC	
989	XP 6678	AC	
990	XP 6670	AC	
991	XP 8243	B	
992	XP 6668	AC	
993	XP 6649	X	
994	XP 6699	CF	
995	XP 6689	CF	MET
996	XP 6690	AC	
997	XP 8229	Q	MET
998	XP 6700	M	
999	XP 8230	Q	
1000	XP 8207	AC	
1001	XP 6693	AC	
1002	XP 8201	AC	MET
1003	XP 8217	AC	MET
1004	XP 6697	M	
1005	XP 6671	AC	MET
1006	XP 8202	CF	
1007	XP 8274	BK	
1008	XP 8203	M	
1009	XP 6679	AC	MET
1010	XP 8266	BK	
1011	XP 8204	Q	
1012	XP 8211	AC	
1013	XP 8220	W	
1014	XP 6694	M	
1015	XP 8218	AC	
1016	XP 8205	AC	MET
1017	XR 1429	AL	
1018	XP 8240	CF	
1019	XP 6692	AC	MET
1020	XP 8226	Q	
1021	XP 8219	AC	
1022	XP 6695	CF	
1023	XP 6698	AC	
1024	NK 6935		NAT
1025	XP XP 8212	B	
1026	XP 8221	B	
1027	XP 8227	Q	
1028	NK 7047		NAT
1029	XP 8208	B	
1030	XP 8231	Q	
1031	XP 8213	B	MET
1032	XP 8244	CF	
1033	NK 6919		NAT
1034	XP 8209	BK	
1035	XP 8241	CF	
1036	NK 6918		NAT
1037	XP 8214	AC	MET

NS	Reg No.	Garage	Remark
1038	NK 6936		NAT
1039	XP 8222	Q	
1040	XP 8223	CF	
1041	XP 8215	B	
1042	XP 8224	Q	MET
1043	XP 8216	CF	MET
1044	XP 8275	B	
1045	XR 1445	AL	
1046	XP 8232	Q	
1047	NK 6953		NAT
1048	XP 8297	W	
1049	XP 8276	CF	
1050	XP 8234	B	
1051	XR 1412	BK	
1052	XP 8237	Q	
1053	NK 7048		NAT
1054	XP 8235	CF	
1055	XP 8285	BK	
1056	XP 8236	B	
1057	XP 8277	CF	
1058	XP 8278	CF	
1059	XP 8286	BK	
1060	XP 8250	B	
1061	XR 1446	AL	
1062	XP 8242	B	
1063	XP 8258	CF	MET
1064	XP 8245	CF	
1065	XP 8251	B	
1066	XP 8252	B	
1067	XP 8246	B	MET
1068	XP 8267	B	
1069	XP 8253	CF	
1070	XP 8268	B	
1071	XP 8254	B	
1072	NK 6989		NAT
1073	XP 8247	B	
1074	XP 8259	B	
1075	XP 8287	B	
1076	XP 8270	BK	
1077	XP 8260	B	
1078	XP 8255	B	
1079	XP 8271	B	
1080	XP 8248	CF	
1081	XP 8261	B	
1082	XP 8273	CF	
1083	XP 8249	B	
1084	XP 8256	B	
1085	XP 8300	AE	
1086	XR 1440	AL	
1087	XP 8288	N	
1088	XR 1447	AL	
1089	XP 8257	CF	
1090	XP 8269	AL	
1091	XP 8262	B	
1092	XR 1448	B	
1093	NK 7367		NAT
1094	NK 6990		NAT
1095	XP 8289	W	
1096	XP 8290	B	
1097	XP 8263	B	
1098	XR 1430	AL	

NS	Reg No.	Garage	Remark	NS	Reg No.	Garage	Remark	NS	Reg No.	Garage	Remark
1099	XP 8264	CF		1160	XR 1479	CF		1221	XR 4236	B	
1100	NK 7363		NAT	1161	XR 1409	BK		1222	XR 1469	AL	
1101	XP 8291	W		1162	NK 7364		NAT	1223	XR 1459	P	
1102	XP 8292	B		1163	XR 1410	BK		1224	XR 4247	AC	
1103	XR 1438	AL	MET	1164	XR 1444	B		1225	XR 1499	P	MET
1104	NK 7049		NAT	1165	XR 1411	BK		1226	XR 1470	AE	
1105	XR 1449	AL		1166	XR 4265	J		1227	XR 1471	AE	
1106	XR 1403	AE		1167	XR 1480	AE		1228	XR 4263	AC	
1107	XP 8293	W		1168	XR 1417	BK		1229	XR 1500	D	
1108	XR 1404	AE	MET	1169	XR 1463	AL		1230	XR 4230	AL	
1109	XP 8265	B		1170	XR 1434	AL		1231	XR 4231	B	
1110	XP 8294	B		1171	XR 1418	BK		1232	XR 4213	CF	
1111	XR 1450	AL		1172	XR 1419	BK		1233	XR 4201	D	
1112	XR 1439	AL		1173	XR 1464	AL		1234	XR 4237	B	
1113	XR 1405	AE	MET	1174	XR 4208	D		1235	XR 1472	AE	
1114	XP 8298	W		1175	XR 1420	BK		1236	XR 4214	CF	
1115	XP 8299	W		1176	XR 1465	AL		1237	XR 4238	AL	MET
1116	XR 1451	AL		1177	XR 1455	AE		1238	XR 4202	B	
1117	XR 1401	W		1178	XR 1490	CF		1239	XR 4215	CF	
1118	XP 8272	B		1179	XR 1481	AE		1240	XR 4216	P	
1119	XP 8233	CF		1180	XR 1466	AE	MET	1241	XR 4221	CF	
1120	XR 1431	AL		1181	XR 1435	AL		1242	XR 4239	B	
1121	XP 8295	BK		1182	XR 1482	D		1243	XR 4222	CF	
1122	XR 1421	BK		1183	XR 1425	AL		1244	XR 4223	P	
1123	XR 1473	BP		1184	XR 4209	B		1245	XR 4224	P	
1124	XP 8280	CF		1185	XR 1483	CF		1246	XR 4248	AC	
1125	XR 1422	BK		1186	XR 1491	D		1247	XR 4275	J	
1126	XP 8284	BK		1187	XR 1492	CF		1248	XR 4246	AK	
1127	XP 8281	B		1188	XR 1484	B		1249	XR 4203	CF	
1128	XR 1413	BK		1189	XR 1426	BK	MET	1250	XR 4241	B	
1129	XR 4205	AE		1190	XR 1485	D	MET	1251	XR 4267	AE	
1130	XP 8282	B		1191	XR 4274	AL		1252	XR 4295	AK	
1131	XR 1441	AL		1192	XR 4210	AL		1253	XR 4204	CF	
1132	XR 1432	AE		1193	XR 1462	AL		1254	XR 4225	CF	
1133	XP 8283	W		1194	XR 1456	AL		1255	XR 1232	P	
1134	XP 8296	W	MET	1195	XR 1493	D		1256	XR 4226	D	
1135	XR 1475	D		1196	XR 4227	B		1257	XR 4242	P	
1136	XR 1414	BK		1197	XR 4211	D		1258	XR 4233	B	
1137	XR 1476	CF		1198	XR 1494	CF		1259	XR 4249	AC	
1138	XR 4206	CF		1199	XR 1427	BK	MET	1260	XR 4234	B	
1139	XR 1452	AL		1200	XR 4212	CF		1261	XR 4243	B	
1140	XR 1415	BK		1201	XR 1428	AL		1262	XR 4235	B	
1141	XR 1460	AE		1202	XR 1495	D		1263	XR 4268	J	
1142	XR 1443	AL		1203	XR 1436	AL		1264	XR 4276	J	
1143	XR 1406	AE		1204	XR 4228	B		1265	XR 4250	P	
1144	XR 1416	CF		1205	XR 1457	AL		1266	XR 9909	D	
1145	XR 1407	BK		1206	XU 6148	E		1267	XR 4251	P	
1146	XR 1477	AE		1207	XR 1437	AE		1268	XR 4217	AE	
1147	XR 1423	AE		1208	XR 1467	AL		1269	XR 4218	CF	
1148	XR 1478	AE		1209	XR 1486	D		1270	XR 4244	B	
1149	NK 7366		NAT	1210	XR 4219	P		1271	XR 4296	AK	
1150	XR 1424	CF		1211	XR 1496	CF		1272	XR 4269	AL	
1151	XR 1474	D		1212	XR 4229	P		1273	XR 4245	P	
1152	XR 1461	AL		1213	XR 4220	AL		1274	XR 4252	AC	
1153	XR 1433	AL		1214	XR 1487	CF		1275	XR 4253	AC	
1154	XR 1453	AL		1215	XR 1497	CF		1276	XR 4254	AK	
1155	XR 1454	AL		1216	XR 1458	AL		1277	XR 4246	B	
1156	XR 4207	CF		1217	XR 4266	J		1278	XR 4255	AC	
1157	XR 1408	AL		1218	XR 1498	D		1279	XR 4297	D	
1158	XR 1489	CF		1219	XR 1488	P		1280	XR 4277	AL	
1159	XR 1402	W		1220	XR 1468	AL		1281	XR 4264	AL	

NS	Reg. No.	Garage	Remark	NS	Reg. No.	Garage	Remark	NS	Reg. No.	Garage	Remark
1282	XR 4256	AC		1343	XR 9956	D		1404	XT 6024	E	
1283	XR 4257	AE		1344	XR 9916	AR		1405	XT 6025	T	
1284	XR 4278	D		1345	XR 9937	AL		1406	XT 6053	J	
1285	XR 4270	AE		1346	XR 9938	T		1407	XT 6054	Q	
1286	XR 4279	J		1347	XR 9939	AR		1408	XT 6076	V	
1287	XR 4271	J		1348	XR 9949	D		1409	XT 6030	T	
1288	XR 4291	AK		1349	XR 9950	AL		1410	XT 6037	Q	
1289	XR 9933	AR		1350	XR 9940	R		1411	XT 6026	BK	
1290	XR 4280	AL		1351	XR 9908	AR		1412	XT 6028	Q	
1291	XR 4298	D		1352	XR 9951	Q		1413	XT 6038	Q	
1292	XR 4281	AK		1353	XR 9952	R		1414	XT 6029	Q	
1293	XR 4258	AE		1354	XR 9957	D		1415	XT 6039	AF	
1294	XR 4283	AK		1355	XR 4288	AL		1416	XT 6040	V	
1295	XR 4292	AK		1356	XR 9955	AL		1417	XT 6046	F	
1296	XR 4284	AK		1357	XR 9963	Q		1418	XT 6031	F	
1297	XR 4282	AK		1358	XR 9958	Q		1419	XT 6055	Q	
1298	XR 4259	P		1359	XR 9959	Q		1420	XT 6043	T	MET
1299	XR 9925	D		1360	XR 9960	BK		1421	XT 6056	Q	
1300	XR 4299	D		1361	XR 9964	BK		1422	XT 6057	Q	
1301	XR 4300	D		1362	XT 6006	Q		1423	XT 6089	W	
1302	XR 4260	AC		1363	XT 6007	M		1424	XT 6047	F	
1303	XR 9900	D		1364	XR 9965	Q		1425	XT 6041	AF	
1304	XR 9910	D		1365	XT 6008	M		1426	XT 6042	T	
1305	XR 9911	AK		1366	XR 9968	BK		1427	XT 6049	AF	
1306	XR 9944	R		1367	XT 6016	M		1428	XT 6044	T	MET
1307	XR 4285	AK		1368	XR 9966	D		1429	XT 6058	T	
1308	XR 4293	AK		1369	XT 6032	T		1430	XT 6082	AF	
1309	XR 4261	AL		1370	XR 9969	W		1431	XU 1808	S	
1310	XR 4286	AK		1371	XR 9967	D		1432	XT 6060	V	
1311	XR 4272	AC		1372	XT 6017	W		1433	XT 6075	Q	
1312	XR 4294	AK		1373	XT 6033	W		1434	XT 6050	Q	
1313	XR 4262	AC		1374	XT 6034	W		1435	XT 6045	T	
1314	XR 9922	AR		1375	XT 6018	M		1436	XT 6064	T	
1315	XR 4273	AL		1376	XT 6035	R		1437	XT 6051	Q	
1316	XR 9901	AK		1377	XR 9970	W		1438	XT 6067	R	
1317	XR 9902	AK		1378	XR 9973	D		1439	XT 6048	Q	
1318	XR 9903	AK		1379	XR 9971	W		1440	XT 6052	AF	
1319	XR 9904	AK		1380	XT 6036	Q		1441	XT 6059	F	
1320	XR 9923	AR		1381	XT 6001	BK		1442	XT 6068	T	
1321	XR 9928	AR		1382	XR 9972	W		1443	XU 1835	W	MET
1322	XR 9929	AR		1383	XT 6009	Q		1444	XU 1825	S	
1323	XR 9924	AR		1384	XR 9974	D		1445	XT 6090	AR	
1324	XR 9905	AK		1385	XR 9975	Q		1446	XT 6061	J	
1325	XR 9906	AR		1386	XT 6002	M		1447	XT 6069	J	
1326	XR 9912	AK		1387	XR 9976	W		1448	XU 1826	W	
1327	XR 9934	V		1388	XR 9977	T		1449	XT 6062	AF	
1328	XR 9907	AK		1389	XT 6015	M		1450	XT 6077	AR	
1329	XR 9935	R		1390	XT 6010	NK		1451	XT 6063	AF	
1330	XR 9913	AK		1391	XT 6003	W		1452	XT 6070	Q	
1331	XR 9945	R		1392	XT 6004	AF		1453	XT 6071	BK	
1332	XR 9946	V		1393	XT 6005	W		1454	XT 6065	J	
1333	XR 4287	AK		1394	XT 6019	M		1455	XT 6078	Q	
1334	XR 9914	AK		1395	XT 6011	T	MET	1456	XU 1809	F	
1335	XR 9915	AR		1396	XT 6012	J		1457	XU 1846	Q	MET
1336	XR 9930	V		1397	XT 6020	T		1458	XU 1827	S	
1337	XR 9936	AL		1398	XT 6013	M		1459	XT 6072	J	
1338	XR 9947	V		1399	XT 6021	BK		1460	XU 1801	AR	
1339	XR 9948	AL		1400	XT 6022	AR		1461	XT 6079	W	
1340	XR 9931	AR		1401	XT 6014	W		1462	XU 1828	S	
1341	XR 9932	AR		1402	XT 6027	BK		1463	XT 6066	BK	
1342	XR 9962	Q		1403	XT 6023	Q		1464	XU 1810	F	

NS	Reg. No.	Garage	Remark	NS	Reg. No.	Garage	Remark	NS	Reg. No.	Garage	Remark
1465	XT 6080	Q		1526	XU 1840	AR		1587	XU 6109	AL	
1466	XT 6073	Q		1527	XU 1873	T		1588	XU 6143	AQ	
1467	XT 6074	AR	MET	1528	XU 1861	Q		1589	XU 6144	Q	
1468	XU 1805	W	MET	1529	XU 1880	U		1590	XU 6130	Q	
1469	XU 1829	V		1530	XU 1844	Q	MET	1591	XU 6145	CF	
1470	XT 6086	V	MET	1531	XU 1876	T		1592	XU 6116	Q	
1471	XU 1811	F		1532	XU 1881	U		1593	XU 6131	T	
1472	XT 6081	Q		1533	XU 1855	AR		1594	XU 6127	AR	
1473	XT 1830	V		1534	XU 1882	AL		1595	XU 6128	AR	
1474	XT 6085	V		1535	XU 1853	Q		1596	XU 6117	AR	
1475	XU 1812	F		1536	XU 1883	T		1597	XU 6132	T	
1476	XT 6083	AF		1537	XU 1859	U		1598	XU 6118	AR	
1477	XT 6087	AF	MET	1538	XU 1862	U		1599	XU 6110	V	
1478	XT 9088 _6088_	AR		1539	XU 1856	AD		1600	XU 6111	AL	
1479	XT 9084 _6084_	AF		1540	XU 1884	AL		1601	XU 6112	AL	
1480	XU 1802	V		1541	XU 1854	AL	MET	1602	XU 6146	E	
1481	XU 1819	AR		1542	XU 1885	U		1603	XU 6147	AD	
1482	XU 1864	T		1543	XU 1878	U		1604	XU 6119	AL	
1483	XU 1816	R		1544	XU 6104	T		1605	XU 1815	F	
1484	XU 1803	AR		1545	XU 1877	U		1606	XU 6154		NAT
1485	XU 1831	Q	MET	1546	XU 1872	U		1607	XU 6149		NAT
1486	XU 1804	AR		1547	XU 1860	D		1608	NK 8904		NAT
1487	XU 1832	Q		1548	XU 1863	AL	MET	1609	XU 6150	AP	
1488	XU 1813	AF		1549	XU 1890	AL		1610	PD 3470		ESTC
1489	XU 1806	R		1550	XU 1886	T		1611	XU 6152	J	
1490	XU 1865	T		1551	XU 1874	U		1612	NK 8903		NAT
1491	XU 1866	G		1552	XU 1845	Q		1613	XU 6151		NAT
1492	XU 1817	W		1553	XU 1879	U	MET	1614	XU 6153	BK	
1493	XU 1847	Q		1554	XU 1875	D		1615	XU 6155	Q	
1494	NK 8405		NAT	1555	XU 6124	T		1616	NK 9085		NAT
1495	NK 8406		NAT	1556	XU 1857	AD		1617	XU 6166	C	MET
1456	XU 1818	W		1557	XU 1891	T		1618	XU 6162	BK	
1497	XU 1807	V		1558	XU 1887	U		1619	XU 6167	C	
1498	XU 1814	AF		1559	XU 6101	U		1620	XU 6156	T	
1499	XU 1867	T	MET	1560	XU 6133	AR		1621	XU 6157	Q	
1500	NK 8407		NAT	1561	XU 6125	AR		1622	XU 6158	Q	
1501	XU 1820	R		1562	XU 1888	U		1623	XU 6159	T	
1502	XU 1838	W		1563	XU 6105	U		1624	XU 6160	T	
1503	XU 1848	AD	MET	1564	XU 1889	U	MET	1625	XU 6161	T	
1504	XU 1849	U	MET	1565	XU 6120	AL		1626	XU 6168	C	
1505	XU 1836	Q		1566	XU 6126	AR		1627	XU 6163	C	
1506	XU 1833	Q		1567	XU 6102	AL		1628	XU 6164	C	
1507	XU 1858	Q		1568	XU 6108	Q		1629	XU 6165	BK	
1508	XU 1868	Q		1569	XU 6103	U		1630	XU 6169	C	
1509	XU 1837	Q		1570	XU 6106	U		1631	XU 6172	C	
1510	XU 1850	Q		1571	XU 6121	AL		1632	XU 6170	AP	
1511	XU 1821	Q		1572	XU 6107	U		1633	XU 6171	AP	
1512	XU 1851	Q		1573	XU 6134	T		1634	XU 6174	G	
1513	XU 1839	AR		1574	XU 6114	G		1635	XU 6173	C	
1514	XU 1822	S		1575	XU 6135	T		1636	XU 6175	BK	MET
1515	XU 1823	Q	MET	1576	XU 6122	AL		1637	XU 6176	M	
1516	XU 1824	R		1577	XU 6115	AL		1638	XU 6177	BK	
1517	XU 1869	Q	MET	1578	XU 6136	AR		1639	XU 6178	HW	
1518	XU 6113	AL		1579	XU 6137	AR		1640	XU 6179	R	
1519	XU 1870	T	MET	1580	XU 6138	Q		1641	XU 6180	R	
1520	XU 1842	Q		1581	XU 6139	AP		1642	XU 6181	X	
1521	XU 1843	Q		1582	XU 6140	E		1643	XU 6182	R	
1522	XU 1841	W		1583	XU 6141	AR		1644	XU 6183	R	
1523	XU 1852	Q		1584	XU 6129	R		1645	XU 6184	V	
1524	XU 1834	Q		1585	XU 6142	AR		1646	XU 6185	X	
1525	XU 1871	D		1586	XU 6123	AR		1647	XU 6186	S	

NS	Reg No.	Garage	Remark	NS	Reg No.	Garage	Remark	NS	Reg. No.	Garage	Remark
1648	XU 6188	X		1709	XW 9855	CF		1770	YL 8087	AR	
1649	XU 6189	V		1710	XW 9856	CF		1771	YL 8078	AR	
1650	XU 6187	J		1711	RO 571		NAT	1772	YL 8077	AR	
1651	PE 1720		ESTC	1712	XW 9837	AE		1773	YL 8076	AR	
1652	XU 6191	J		1713	XW 9857	CF		1774	YL 8079	AR	
1653	PE 1725		ESTC	1714	XW 9858	CF		1775	YL 8080	AR	
1654	XU 6194	AR		1715	XW 9838	T		1776	YL 8091	AR	
1655	XU 6195	V		1716	XW 9839	T	MET	1777	YL 8081	AR	
1656	XU 6196	X		1717	XW 9841	BK		1778	YL 8083	AR	
1657	XW 9803	T		1718	XW 9842	C		1779	YL 8088	AR	
1658	XU 6197	X		1719	XW 9843	C		1780	YL 8084	AR	
1659	XW 9801	X		1720	XW 9853	C		1781	YL 8089	AR	
1660	PE 1722		ESTC	1721	XW 9844	C		1782	YL 8092	AR	
1661	XW 9802	T		1722	XW 9847	BK		1783	YL 8090	AR	
1662	PE 1721		ESTC	1723	XW 9848	C		1784	YL 8093	AR	
1663	XW 9807	AR		1724	XW 9849	C		1785	YL 8096	AR	
1664	XW 9814	J		1725	XW 9862	CF		1786	YL 8097	AR	
1665	XW 9804	T		1726	XW 9859	CF		1787	YL 8099	AR	
1666	XW 9808	J		1727	XW 9851	K		1788	YL 8100	AR	
1667	XW 9815	J		1728	XW 9852	C		1789	YN 3712	AR	
1668	XW 9809	J		1729	XW 9860	CF		1790	YN 3713	AR	
1669	XW 9810	T		1730	XW 9863	CF		1791	YN 3714	AR	
1670	XW 9811	J		1731	XW 9861	CF		1792	YN 3715	AR	
1671	XW 9812	J		1732	XW 9845	CF		1793	YN 3716	AR	
1672	XW 9816	J		1733	XW 9850	CF		1794	YN 3717	AR	
1673	XW 9817	J		1734	XW 9881	L		1795	YN 3719	AR	
1674	XW 9822	AR		1735	XW 9882	L		1796	YN 3718	AR	
1675	XW 9818	V		1736	XW 9883	L		1797	YN 3722	AR	
1676	XW 9819	C		1737	XW 9884	L		1798	YN 3721	AR	
1677	XW 9823	V		1738	YN 3799			1799	YN 3720	AR	
1678	XW 9828 *26*	J		1739	RO 2676		NAT	1800	YN 3723	AR	
1679	XW 9820	J		1740	RO 3736		NAT	1801	YN 3724	AR	
1680	XW 9821	J		1741	RO 2677		NAT	1802	YN 3725	AR	
1681	PE 1726		ESTC	1742	PE 8824		ESTC	1803	YN 3726	AR	
1682	PE 1723		ESTC	1743	PE 8825		ESTC	1804	YN 3727	AR	
1683	XU 6190	C		1744	YL 8061	R		1805	YN 3728	AR	
1684	PE 1724		ESTC	1745	YL 8062	R		1806	YN 3729	AP	
1685	XW 9827	J		1746	YL 8063	R		1807	YN 3730	AR	
1686	XW 9828	T		1747	PE 8997		ESTC	1808	YN 3731	AP	
1687	XU 6192	T		1748	YL 8065	AR		1809	YN 3732	AR	
1688	XW 9829	V		1749	YL 8066	R		1810	YN 3733	AR	
1689	XW 9805	AR		1750	PE 8998		ESTC	1811	YN 3734	AR	
1690	XW 9831	AR	MET	1751	YL 8067	R		1812	YN 3735	AP	
1691	XW 9806	AE		1752	PE 8999		ESTC	1813	YN 3736	AR	
1692	XW 9824	V		1753	PE 9000		ESTC	1814	YN 3737	AR	
1693	XW 9832	C		1754	YL 8068	R		1815	YN 3738	L	
1694	XW 9830	AE		1755	YL 8069	R		1816	YN 3739	AP	
1695	PE 1728		ESTC	1756	PE 9260		ESTC	1817	YN 3740	L	
1696	PE 1727		ESTC	1757	PE 9082		ESTC	1818	YN 3741	AP	
1697	XW 9833	BK		1758	PE 9180		ESTC	1819	YN 3742	L	
1698	XW 9834	BK		1759	YL 8070	R		1820	YN 3743	L	
1699	XW 9825	AR		1760	YL 8071	R		1821	YN 3744	AP	
1700	XW 9835	AE		1761	PE 9672		ESTC	1822	YN 3745	AP	
1701	XW 9840	C		1762	YL 8072	AR		1823	YN 3746	AP	
1702	XW 9836	AR		1763	YL 8082	AR		1824	YN 3747	AP	
1703	PE 1729		ESTC	1764	PE 9673	AR		1825	YN 3748	L	
1704	XW 9826	C		1765	YL 8073	AR		1826	YN 3749	L	
1705	RO 572		NAT	1766	YL 8085	AR		1827	YN 3750	AP	
1706	RO 205		NAT	1767	YL 8074	AR		1828	YN 3751	AP	
1707	XW 9854	C		1768	YL 8075	AR		1829	YN 3752	AP	
1708	XW 9846	CF		1769	YL 8086	AR		1830	YN 3753	AP	

NS	Reg No.	Garage	Remark	NS	Reg No.	Garage	Remark	NS	Reg. No.	Garage	Remark
1831	YN 3754	D	MET	1892	YP 6644	J		1953	BT 7649	J	
1832	YN 3755	AP		1893	YP 6643	BK		1954	YP 6699	AL	
1833	YN 3756	AP		1894	YP 6645	J		1955	YP 6700	AD	
1834	YN 3757	AP		1895	YP 6646	BK		1956	YR 3801	AD	
1835	YN 3758	AP		1896	YP 6662	D		1957	YR 3802	AL	
1836	YN 3759	D		1897	YP 6651	BK		1958	YR 3803	AD	
1837	YN 3760	AP		1898	YP 6647	BK		1959	YR 3804	M	
1838	YN 3761	AP		1899	YP 6648	BK		1960	YR 3805	AD	
1839	YN 3762	AP		1900	YP 6652	BK		1961	YR 3809	AD	
1840	YN 3763	AP		1901	YP 6653	J		1962	YR 3810	AD	
1841	YN 3764	AP		1902	YP 6654	BK		1963	YR 3811	AD	
1842	YN 3765	AP		1903	YP 6655	J		1964	YR 3812	AD	
1843	YN 3766	AP		1904	YP 6656	D		1965	YR 3813	M	
1844	YN 3767	AP		1905	YP 6657	D		1966	YR 3814	AL	
1845	YN 3768	AP		1906	YP 6658	HW		1967	YR 3815	SL	
1846	YN 3769	AP		1907	YP 6663	BK		1968	YR 3816	AD	
1847	YN 3770	AP		1908	YP 6664	HW		1969	YR 3817	AL	
1848	YN 3771	AP		1909	YP 6665	HW		1970	YR 3819	M	
1849	YN 3772	D		1910	YP 6666	BK		1971	YR 3820	AL	
1850	YN 3773	AP		1911	YP 6667	D		1972	YR 3821	M	
1851	YN 3774	AP		1912	YP 6668	AL		1973	YR 3824	AC	MET
1852	YN 3775	D		1913	YP 6669	F		1974	YR 3825	M	
1853	YN 3776	AP		1914	YP 6670	D		1975	YR 3826	AC	
1854	YN 3777	AP		1915	YP 6671	F		1976	YR 3822	AL	
1855	YN 3778	D	MET	1916	YP 6672	D		1977	YR 3823	M	
1856	YN 3779	G		1917	YP 6673	HW		1978	YR 3827	M	
1857	YN 3780	BK		1918	YP 6674	F		1979	YR 3878	AC	
1858	YN 3781	B		1919	YP 6677	AD		1980	YR 3824	AC	
1859	YN 3782	D	MET	1920	YP 6678	AD		1981	YR 3830	J	
1860	YN 3783	BK		1921	YP 6679	HW		1982	YR 3831	AC	
1861	YN 3784	BK	MET	1922	YP 6680	AD		1983	YR 3832	AC	MET
1862	YP 6611	B		1923	YP 6681	F		1984	YR 3833	M	
1863	YP 6601	G		1924	YP 6682	AL		1985	YR 3834	AC	MET
1864	YP 6602	D		1925	YP 6683	F		1986	YR 3835	W	
1865	YP 6612	G		1926	YP 6685	AL		1987	YR 3836	AC	MET
1866	YP 6613	B		1927	YP 6686	HW		1988	YR 3837	AC	MET
1867	YP 6614	B		1928	YP 6687	AL		1989	YR 3838	AC	MET
1868	YP 6615	J		1929	YP 6688	HW		1990	YR 3839	AC	
1869	YP 6616	B		1930	YP 6689	HW		1991	YR 3840	W	
1870	YP 6603	D	MET	1931	YP 6690	HW		1992	YR 3841	AC	MET
1871	YP 6604	BK		1932	YP 6691	AL		1993	YR 3842	AC	
1872	YP 6605	BK		1933	YP 6692	AD		1994	YR 3843	J	
1873	YP 6617	B		1934	YP 6694	AD		1995	YR 3844	G	
1874	YP 6618	B		1935	YP 6695	AD		1996	YR 3845	AC	
1875	YP 6619	BK		1936	YP 6696	AD		1997	YR 3846	J	
1876	YP 6620	G		1937	YP 6697	AD		1998	YR 3847	AC	
1877	YP 6622	B		1938	YP 6698	AL		1999	YR 3848	W	
1878	YP 6626	B		1939	YL 8094	G		2000	YR 3849	J	
1879	YP 6627	J		1940	YL 8095	G		2001	YR 3850	J	
1880	YP 6628	BK		1941	YL 8098	G		2002	YR 3851	W	
1881	YP 6629	BK		1942	YN 3703	G		2003	YR 3852	W	
1882	YP 6630	BK		1943	YN 3704	CF		2004	YR 3853	B	
1883	YP 6631	BK		1944	YN 3701	AV		2005	YR 3854	W	
1884	YP 6635	B		1945	YN 3702	AV		2006	YR 3855	W	
1885	YP 6636	B		1946	YN 3706	G		2007	YR 3856	W	
1886	YP 6637	B		1947	YN 3705	G		2008	YR 3857	B	
1887	YP 6638	B		1948	YN 3707	AV		2009	YR 3858	W	
1888	YP 6639	B		1949	YN 3708	G		2010	YR 3859	W	
1889	YP 6640	D		1950	YN 3709	G	MET	2011	YR 3860	W	
1890	YP 6641	J		1951	YN 3711	G		2012	YR 3861	W	
1891	YP 6642	D		1952	YN 3710	G		2013	YR 3862	W	

NS	Reg No.	Garage	Remark	NS	Reg No.	Garage	Remark	NS	Reg. No.	Garage	Remark
2014	YR 3863	AL		2075	YE 4337	T		2136	YH 1151	T	
2015	YR 3864	HW		2076	YE 4338	AR		2137	YH 1152	HW	
2016	YR 3865	H		2077	YE 4339	AD		2138	YH 1153	HW	
2017	YR 3866	AL		2078	YE 4340	AD		2139	YH 1154	HW	
2018	YR 3868	T		2079	YE 4341	AD		2140	YH 1155	HW	
2019	YR 3867	W		2080	YE 4342	AD		2141	YH 1156	T	
2020	YR 3869	W		2081	YE 4343	H		2142	YH 1157	T	
2021	YR 3870	W		2082	YE 4344	AD		2143	YH 1158	HW	
2022	YR 3871	W		2083	YE 4345	AD		2144	YH 1159	HW	
2023	YR 3872	W		2084	YE 4346	AD		2145	YH 1160	HW	
2024	YR 3873	W		2085	YE 4347	AC		2146	YH 1161	HW	
2025	YR 3874	W		2086	YE 4348	AD		2147	YH 1162	HW	
2026	YR 3878	W		2087	YE 4349	H		2148	YH 1163	HW	
2027	YR 3879	AE		2088	YE 4350	AC		2149	YH 1164	HW	
2028	YR 3880	AL		2089	YE 4351	AC		2150	YH 1165	HW	
2029	YR 3892	CF		2090	YE 4352	AC		2151	YT 4801	T	
2030	YR 3893	H		2091	YE 4353	AC		2152	YT 4802	HW	
2031	YR 3894	H		2092	YE 4354	AC		2153	YT 4803	HW	
2032	YR 3895	H		2093	YE 4355	AC		2154	YT 4804	HW	
2033	YR 3896	AE		2094	YE 4356	AC		2155	YT 4805	AM	
2034	YR 3897	H		2095	YE 4357	AC		2156	YT 4806	HW	
2035	YR 3898	B		2096	YE 4358	AC		2157	YT 4807	HW	
2036	YE 4301	AE		2097	YE 4359	H		2158	YT 4808	HW	
2037	YE 4303	AE		2098	YE 4360	H		2159	YT 4809	L	
2038	YE 4302	H		2099	YH 1114	G		2160	YT 4810	L	
2039	YE 4304	CF		2100	YH 1115	G		2161	YT 4811	L	
2040	YE 4305	H		2101	YH 1116	AR		2162	YT 4812	AM	
2041	YE 4309	T		2102	YH 1117	AR		2163	YT 4813	AM	
2042	YE 4306	H		2103	YH 1118	AR		2164	YT 4814	AM	
2043	YE 4307	H		2104	YH 1119	W		2165	YT 4815	AM	
2044	YE 4310	CF		2105	YH 1120	W		2166	YT 4816	AM	
2045	YE 4308	CF		2106	YH 1121	W		2167	YT 4817	AM	
2046	YE 4311	AD		2107	YH 1122	V		2168	YT 4818	W	
2047	YE 4312	AD		2108	YH 1123	AK		2169	YT 4819	AM	
2048	YE 4313	AD		2109	YH 1124	Q		2170	YT 4820	W	
2049	YE 4314	AD		2110	YH 1125	AE		2171	YT 4821	AM	
2050	YE 4315	C		2111	YH 1126	T		2172	YT 4822	AM	
2051	HU 8157			2112	YH 1127	Q		2173	YT 4823	W	
2052	HU 8158			2113	YH 1128	Q		2174	YT 4824	AM	
2053	HU 8159			2114	YH 1129	AK		2175	YT 4825	AM	
2054	YE 4316	Q		2115	YH 1130	AK		2176	YT 4826	W	
2055	YE 4317	T		2116	YH 1131	Q		2177	YT 4827	AM	
2056	YE 4318	T		2117	YH 1132	Q		2178	YT 4828	AM	
2057	YE 4319	T		2118	YH 1133	Q		2179	YT 4829	J	
2058	YE 4320	T		2119	YH 1134	Q		2180	YT 4830	J	
2059	YE 4321	T		2120	YH 1135	AK		2181	YT 4841	BK	
2060	YE 4322	T		2121	YH 1136	AK		2182	YT 4832	J	
2061	YE 4323	T		2122	YH 1137	AE		2183	YT 4833	W	
2062	YE 4324	AR		2123	YH 1138	AE		2184	YT 4834	L	
2063	YE 4325	AR		2124	YH 1139	AE		2185	YT 4835	W	
2064	YE 4326	T		2125	YH 1140	AE		2186	YT 4836	L	
2065	YE 4327	AR		2126	YH 1141	AE		2187	YT 4837	L	
2066	YE 4328	T		2127	YH 1142	AE		2188	YT 4838	L	
2067	YE 4329	T		2128	YH 1143	AE		2189	YT 4839	AH	
2068	YE 4330	T		2129	YH 1144	HW		2190	YT 4840	L	
2069	YE 4331	T		2130	YH 1145	HW		2191	YT 4841	X	
2070	YE 4332	AD		2131	YH 1146	T		2192	YT 4842	L	
2071	YE 4333	AD		2132	YH 1147	HW		2193	YT 4843	X	
2072	YE 4334	T		2133	YH 1148	T		2194	YT 4844	L	
2073	YE 4335	T		2134	YH 1149	HW		2195	YT 4845	L	
2074	YE 4336	T		2135	YH 1150	HW		2196	YT 4846	X	

NS	Reg No.	Garage	Remark
2197	YT 4847	X	
2198	YT 4848	X	
2199	YT 4849	X	
2200	YT 4850	AH	
2201	YT 4851	AH	
2202	YT 4852	X	
2203	YT 4853	X	
2204	YT 4854	HW	
2205	YT 4855	X	
2206	YT 4856	X	
2207	YT 4857	Q	
2208	YT 4858	AH	
2209	YT 4859	Q	
2210	YT 4860	C	
2211	YT 4861	Q	
2212	YT 4862	C	
2213	YT 4863	C	
2214	YT 4864	C	
2215	YT 4865	J	
2216	YT 4866	C	
2217	YT 4867	C	
2218	YT 4868	C	
2219	YT 4869	AH	
2220	YT 4870	C	
2221	YT 4871	C	
2222	YT 4872	C	
2223	YT 4873	C	
2224	YT 4874	C	
2225	YT 4875	C	
2226	YT 4876	C	
2227	YT 4877	C	
2228	YT 4878	C	
2229	YR 3875	W	
2230	YW 7983	W	
2231	WU 6715	G	
2232	YT 4880	C	
2233	YT 1881	C	
2234	YT 4882	C	
2235	YT 4883	C	
2236	YT 4884	C	
2237	YT 4885	C	
2238	YT 4886	C	
2239	YT 4887	C	
2240	YT 4888	AH	
2241	YU 6225	HW	
2242	YT 4890	G	
2243	YT 4891	Q	
2244	YT 4892	Q	
2245	YT 4879	G	
2246	YT 4889	G	
2247	YT 4893	G	
2248	YT 4894	R	
2249	YU 6202	R	
2250	YU 6203	R	
2251	YU 6204	R	
2252	YU 6205	R	
2253	YU 6206	R	
2254	YU 6210	AR	
2255	YU 6211	AR	
2256	YU 6212	AR	
2257	YT 4895	R	

NS	Reg No.	Garage	Remark
2258	YT 4896	R	
2259	YT 4897	R	
2260	YU 6201	R	
2261	YU 6207	AR	
2262	YU 6208	V	
2263	YU 6209	V	
2264	YU 6213	AH	
2265	YU 6214	AH	
2266	YU 6215	AH	
2267	YU 6216	AR	
2268	YU 6217	AR	
2269	YU 6218	AR	
2270	YU 6219	J	
2271	YU 6220	J	
2272	YU 6221	J	
2273	YU 6222	F	
2274	YU 6223	F	
2275	YU 6224	F	
2276	YU 6227	W	
2277	YU 6228	W	
2278	UC 2202	AC	
2279	UC 2257	HW	
2280	UC 2258	W	
2281	UC 2259	W	
2282	UC 2260	W	
2283	UC 2262	W	
2284	UC 2263		NAT
2285	UC 2264		NAT
2286	UC 2273	W	
2287	UC 2274	W	
2288	UC 2275	W	
2289	UC 2276	W	
2290	GC 3953	AH	
2291	UC 2277	W	
2292	UC 2278	W	
2293	UC 2279	W	
2294	UC 2280	W	
2295	UC 2281	W	
2296	UC 2282	AR	
2297	UC 2284	W	
2298	YW 9751	M	
2299	UC 2283	W	
2300	UC 2285	W	
2301	UC 2296	W	
2302	YW 7952	W	
2303	YW 7953	M	
2304	UC 2297	W	
2305	UC 2286	W	
2306	YW 7966	M	
2307	UC 2287	W	
2308	YW 7954	M	
2309	YW 7968	M	
2310	YW 7955	M	
2311	UC 2288	W	
2312	YW 7980	M	
2313	YW 7981	M	
2314	YW 7974	M	
2315	UC 2298	W	
2316	UC 2289	W	
2317	UC 2290	W	
2318	UC 2291	W	

NS	Reg. No.	Garage	Remark
2319	YU 6226	W	
2320	UC 2292	W	
2321	UC 2293	W	
2322	UC 2294	W	
2323	YW 7956	W	
2324	YW 7975	M	
2325	YW 7957	M	
2326	UC 2295	M	
2327	YW 7969	M	
2328	YW 7958	M	
2329	YW 7959	M	
2330	YW 7976	M	
2331	YW 7977	M	
2332	YW 7970	M	
2333	YW 7960	M	
2334	YW 7961	M	
2335	YW 7962	W	
2336	YW 7978	M	
2337	YW 7963	W	
2338	YW 7971	M	
2339	YW 7972	M	
2340	YW 7973	M	
2341	YW 7964	W	
2342	YW 7984	W	
2343	YW 7965	W	
2344	YW 7982	M	
2345	YW 7979	M	
2346	YW 7967	M	
2347	PE 2427		
2348	PE 2421		
2349	PE 2424		
2350 to 2371 Cancelled Order			
2372	YW 8042	W	
2373	YW 8033	W	
2374	YW 8040	W	
2375	YW 8041	W	
2376	YW 8034	W	
2377	YW 8043	W	
2378	MP 1460		
2379	YH 1197		
2380	YH 1190		
2381	YH 1198		
2382	YH 1180		
2383	YH 1181		
2384	YH 1193		
2385	YH 1178		
2386	YH 1187		
2387	YH 1195		
2388	YH 1179		
2389	YH 1199		
2390	YH 1191		
2391	YH 1188		
2392	YH 1185		
2393	YH 1194		
2934	YH 1192		
2395	YH 1183		
2396	YH 1186		
2397	YH 1196		
2398	YH 1182		
2399	YH 1189		
2400	YH 1184		

NS	Reg No.	Garage	Remark	NS	Reg No.	Garage	Remark	LS	Reg. No.	Garage	Remark
2401	YH 1176							1	YH 1200	W	
2402	YH 1174			**EAST SURREY NS**				2	YU 1166	W	
2403	YH 1175			2348	PE 2420	162		3	UC 2201	W	
2404	YH 1172				PE 2421	161		4	UC 2255	AD	
2405	YH 1173				PE 2422	163		5	UC 2246	M	
2406	YH 1177				PE 2423	160		6	UC 2299	W	
2407	YH 1169			2349	PE 2424	164		7	UC 2266	M	
2408	YH 1168				PE 2425	165		8	YW 7989	M	
2408	YH 1179				PE 2426	167		9	YW 7985	AR	
2410	YH 1171			2347	PE 2427	166		10	YW 7986	AR	
2411	YH 1167							11	YW 7988	AR	
								12	YW 8003	M	

Note
NK and RO registered buses for National
2347-2349, 2378 Ex East Surrey
2379-2411 Ex British

NS1612 is working out of Watford High Street garage uncoded in "National" and London General Country Services days. It was delivered new to Ware (Town Hall) garage in November 1924 transferring to Watford High Street in October 1929.